Jewish Magic

Unlocking Everything You Need to Know about Jewish Spirituality, Mysticism, and Angels

Free Bonus from Silvia Hill available for limited time

Hi Spirituality Lovers!

My name is Silvia Hill, and first off, I want to THANK YOU for reading my book.

Now you have a chance to join my exclusive spirituality email list so you can get the ebooks below for free as well as the potential to get more spirituality ebooks for free! Simply click the link below to join.

P.S. Remember that it's 100% free to join the list.

$27 FREE BONUSES

- 9 Types of Spirit Guides and How to Connect to Them
- How to Develop Your Intuition: 7 Secrets for Psychic Development and Tarot Reading
- Tarot Reading Secrets for Love, Career, and General Messages

Access your free bonuses here
https://livetolearn.lpages.co/jewish-magic-paperback/

Table of Contents

Introduction

This book is a comprehensive resource on Jewish spirituality, mysticism, and angels. If you've always wanted to learn about Jewish magic but needed to figure out where to begin, this is it. You might be interested in your Hebrew heritage, full of mystical magic. Or you may simply be interested in those aspects of occult knowledge rooted in Jewish spirituality or the Qabalah and want to learn as much as possible on the topic. It could be that you're just interested in starting your spiritual journey, and this is the path calling you the most. Whatever the case, you'll find the information you need on these pages.

Unlike other books on the market, this book is written clearly in plain English with no typos or grammatical errors, so there's no chance you'll misinterpret or misunderstand the message. You will not be left confused and scratching your head about what the concepts mean. By reading this book, you get the chance to look through expert eyes, get an accurate take on Jewish mysticism and spirituality, and dive into their rich history. You'll also be provided with daily routines and practices you can use to help you make the concepts very practical and real in your life. In addition, the writing is inclusive and respectful of cultural and ethnic backgrounds and gender.

This book is a beautiful resource because you'll get information far beyond what you'll find on the internet. It doesn't just dabble in the basics but dives deep into the treasures held in Jewish mysticism's depths. You'll appreciate the many fascinating things about Jewish magic as you read. It's not easy to find books written in English that cover the history of Hebrews and their practices, so you can consider this one a great find – an exceptional read compared to other books on the market!

There's much to explore in the world of Jewish magic and much that will change your life for the better in ways you couldn't possibly have anticipated. That's why your decision to choose this book, learn what it has to offer, and implement it in your life will serve you greatly. Many choose to flounder through life, never questioning it, never looking for meaning and purpose. You, dear reader, are clearly different. You recognize there's so much more to existence than meets the eye, and you've clearly taken the bold step to explore your spirituality.

Now, as you open this book to read, your path will open and light up for you to walk in it. If you're ready to connect to the power that lies in the secrets of Jewish mysticism, and you're ready to leave the person you are behind for a grander version of yourself, let's begin this journey with an introduction to Jewish mysticism and spirituality.

Chapter One: Jewish Mysticism and Spirituality 101

Judaism is one of the oldest religions in the world, focusing on serving just one God. It begins as far back as 4,000 years, at least. Those who subscribe to this religion believe that God made himself known through the prophets of old. To understand Jewish mysticism, you must understand the history. There's much to cover regarding tradition, culture, and law.

Judaism is one of the oldest religions.

For the Jewish people, there's only one God, and God entered into a binding agreement with them, so they are God's chosen ones. God reaches out to those who believe in him through his prophets, rewarding those who do well and giving those who don't do well their due. Traditionally, being Jewish is passed down through the matriarchs of the family, which means if your mom is Jewish, so are you. If you're going to be a practicing Jew, you have to know about and study the *Tanakh,* which is the Hebrew Bible. This text is as sacred as the Quran to Muslims or the Bible to Christians. There are similarities between the Tanakh and the Christian Bible, specifically the Old Testament. Among the most important books of the Hebrew Bible are the collection known as the Torah, which is the first five books – or the *Pentateuch.* They are considered very important because they all have the important laws that one must follow if they are born or decide to be a Jew. What is one of the most important tenets of being a Jew? Judaism involves the belief that the Messiah will one day arrive to save his people. To serve God, you have to attend services at the synagogue, and the rabbi leads each service. Judaism is a way of life that is heavy with symbolism, and perhaps one of the most notable symbols is the six-pointed Star of David, which is universally recognized as Jewish. There's nearly nowhere you can't find Jews, as there are at least 14 million of them across all nations! Mostly, many of them are in their homeland, Israel. The only other place that is as populated by Jews as Israel is the United States of America.

Origins

Abraham was a Hebrew from the Old Testament times. However, he was no ordinary Hebrew; he was the one to whom God chose to reveal himself. Not only *that,* he was the one God made a remarkable promise: Abraham would be the father of all nations. That was a promise God made good on!

Abraham is the one who is, according to the Torah, who premiered the faith of Judaism. God entered into a contract or covenant with Abraham, promising that he and his offspring would become a powerful nation. Abraham had a son named Isaac and a grandson named Jacob. These three would go on to become very important personalities in Jewish history. Eventually, Jacob would take on a new name: Israel. The name Israel means "God contended," and he got that name after wrestling with an angel standing in for Yahweh. Obviously, wrestling with an angel was no mean feat, but somehow, Jacob could pull it off and survive. It's known that battling with God is a daily experience as you struggle with the process of asking questions and studying more, all to understand the great Ein Sof, and to find meaning in your life. Being a Jew doesn't mean you swallow everything you're taught hook, line, and sinker. You have to think about what you're being told of God for you to meet God within yourself. Just because you have questions about the things you learn about God doesn't make you a bad Jew. It took a thousand years after Abraham's time for the people of Israel to finally win their freedom from the tough enslavement of the Egyptians, and they couldn't have done this without God's help. He was able to rescue them through his holy servant, Moses. It was through Moses that the Oral Torah or Oral Law was made known to the Israelites, as God told Moses everything the people needed to know on Mount Sinai. The Jews have had some tough times all through history, with some events being so ugly that it was evident the faith and its details were in danger of being obliterated on account of systemic persecution. So a certain Rabbi known as Judah the Prince decided not to let that happen, and he wrote down everything of the Oral Torah in the Mishnah. The Mishnah is the first main collection of Jewish oral traditions that were penned down and the very first important work in rabbinic literature.

There are two very important figures in the history of Israel and Judaism: David and his son Solomon. David was the King of Israel at a certain point in time, and his son was the one who built the first Temple of Jerusalem, which was no mean feat. This meant that the Israelites finally had a formal place of worship where they could serve God. However, this Temple wasn't meant to last, as the kingdom of Israel would come to an end eventually. This meant that Israelites were now divided into two camps. In the North were Israelites, and in the South were the people of Judah. This split in the kingdom came around 931 BC, with the destruction of the first Temple happening in 587 BC. The Babylonians swooped in and destroyed everything the Israelites loved about their temple, and as if that weren't enough, they had to exile them as well. 71 years later, there would be a Second Temple, which only lasted a few centuries. Once more, the people were attacked, and their beloved place of worship was desecrated and destroyed, this time by the Romans. By 70 AD, the Second Temple was no more. This was a landmark event because it meant the Jews had nowhere to gather in worship, so they opted to continue their services in the local synagogues.

Historically, Jews have often been persecuted because of their beliefs. The following are some of the most terrible persecutions that they've had to endure:

- **The Granada Massacre of 1066:** The Granada Royal palace was situated in the Taifa of Granada. This was the place that a mob of Muslim faithfuls decided to break into. Joseph ha-Nagid was the Jewish vizier at the time, working with Berber taifa king Badis al-Muzaffar as, at the time, the Moors reigned over Al-Andalus, and the mob made sure to crucify him because he was the religious head of the Jews in the area. At the time, Spain was under the rulership of Muslims, specifically the Zirid dynasty. It is believed that Jews were in Granada ever since the First Temple was destroyed, and in fact, the place was once called Garnata-al-Yahud, which means Granada, the City of Jews. The Muslims were simply unhappy with the prosperity of the Jewish community at the time,

- **The First Crusade:** During this terrible event, crusaders made their way to Jerusalem, attacking the Jews they encountered as they went through Rhineland and the areas around Heidelberg. The crusaders made sure the Jews had only one of two options: Death or conversion. So many Jews were forced to end their lives with their own hands because they didn't want to betray God or their ways. This was just one in a series of anti-Semitic attacks that would build up to the Holocaust.

- **The Spanish Expulsion:** In 1492 royal edict issued by the Spaniard rulers said all Jews who wouldn't become Christians would be forced out of the country. They followed through on that threat, as about 200,000 Jews were expelled, and tens of thousands died trying to find somewhere safe to escape.

- **The Holocaust:** This is one of the most disastrous of events, as 6 million Jews were murdered in cold blood by the Nazis.

The Different Movements in Judaism

There are variations in the practice of Judaism, most of which are originally from Rabbinic Judaism. Here are the important movements to note.

Pharisaic Judaism is practiced by Pharisees, who had a movement in the Levant during the epoch of Second Temple Judaism. When the Second Temple was destroyed, the beliefs of the Pharisees made up the basis for Rabbinic Judaism.

Rabbinic Judaism is also known as Rabbinicism or Rabbinism. It's been the main form of Judaism since the 6th century CE, once the Babylonian Talmud. These Jews believe that Moses received God's Oral Torah and Written Torah. This form of Judaism holds the Oral Torah in high esteem, unlike the Sadducees, Samaritans, and Karaite Jews.

The Sadducees do not accept the Oral Torah but the Written Torah only. They believe there's no fate and God is incapable of committing evil. They also believe that man has free will, immortality doesn't exist, and there's no afterlife. They also don't believe in being rewarded or punished after death, nor in the resurrection of the dead.

Hellenistic Judaism is a combination of Greek culture and Jewish religious tradition. This was popular in Antioch, Syria, and Alexandria, Egypt, before the Muslim conquests happened.

Karaism or Karaite Judaism recognizes only the written Torah, and they have the Sevel Ha Yerushah, which is "the Yoke of Inheritance," which they have always passed down from the time of their ancestors till now.

Orthodox Judaism teaches that the rabbinical interpretations of the Torah are to be followed to the letter. There are over 600 rules meant to show Orthodox Jews how to comport themselves daily.

Conservative Judaism holds that the Jewish law and tradition have authority thanks to the people and the community, stemming from generations of accepted practices and not rooted in the divine revelation of the Torah.

Hasidic Judaism has followers known as the Hasidim, which means "the pious ones." It took over Eastern Europe to the point that at least half of the Jews in the region were Hasidic. This movement was led by

Yisroel ben Eliezer, or Ba'al Shem Tov. Unfortunately, many Hasidic Jews were massacred during the Holocaust. Hasidic Judaism is a form of Judaism that arose when the Jews were persecuted. At this time, the Jews of Europe turned toward studying the Talmud for themselves and felt like Judaism was being viewed only mostly through academic lenses, taking away from the spiritual aspect of it that makes it a joy to practice. They would gather in small groups, and these meetings took place in a shtiebel – a house of prayer. Here, they could worship and celebrate and socialize with one another.

Reform Judaism is also called Liberal Judaism or Progressive Judaism. This form acknowledges that faith is ever-evolving, and it is more about the ethics of the religion than the ceremony. Those practicing this form of Judaism believe that divine truth is constantly revealed and involves human logic. In other words, it's not just about the theophany Moses experienced on Mount Sinai. It doesn't belabor rituals and considers the body of Jewish laws or halakha optional.

An Overview of Jewish Spirituality

Judaism is rooted in the belief that there is only one God and that God cares what we do as humans. Remember, Abraham had been promised that he'd be the father of all nations, and since this promise was made by God himself, there was no way it would be broken. Since the people that sprung from Abraham's lineage were a direct consequence of the promise, God only wanted one thing from them, and that was for them to worship him. For the Jew, worshipping God is about being a caretaker for all of life in the same way God is a caretaker for the world he created. God told them they had to love one another the same way he loves the world. These two commandments are the major ones God requires the Israelites to follow, but there are other commandments and laws that they have to abide by to keep up their end of the covenant that he had with their forefather, Abraham. This covenant is what acts as the root of Judaism. There is an esoteric aspect to Judaism that some regard as everyday mysticism, and it is known as Kabbalah. Kabbalah is about the way you personally relate with God working with natural Jewish methods by observing the halakha, which is Jewish law. It's also about observing the Birkat Ha-Mitzvot, so that the Jew can become so close to God as to become one with him. The halakha is meant to be a way to help Jews get closer to God and draw the world closer to his divine power.

The Torah

The Torah.

Torah means "Law," "Instruction," or "Teaching." The first five books of the Hebrew Bible are what make up the Torah. The books are:

- Genesis
- Exodus
- Leviticus
- Numbers
- Deuteronomy

Since there are five books in the Torah, it is also known as the Pentateuch. It's also called the Written Torah, in the form of a scroll when it's used liturgically (as the Sefer Torah). The Torah is also known as the Chumash when it's in the form of a bound book, and it will often come with perushim, which are commentaries from Rabis.

Sometimes, Torah can represent the entirety of the Tanakh or the Hebrew Bible. In this case, one refers not just to the Pentateuch but all

24 books. Torah can also sometimes represent everything about Jewish culture, teaching, and practice, including texts from the Bible and inserts from Rabbis, which make up the Oral Torah. It is hard to have an unequivocal definition of the Torah since there are infinite faces to it and myriad ways to interpret it.

Mitzvah

In Jewish tradition, bar and bat mitzvah rituals mark the coming of age. Boys have bar mitzvah, while girls have bat mitzvah. The plural form is known as b'nei mitzvah, and when the ceremony is meant for more than one gender, that's what it's called. If it's only girls involved, then the correct term is b'not mitzvah. What is the essence of this event? It marks the fact that the parents are no longer held accountable for their children's thoughts, words, and actions, since they are now old enough to make their own choices and deal with the outcomes. When Jewish kids are that age, they become a bat mitzvah or bar mitzvah and are therefore responsible for their actions. Usually, the father of a bat mitzvah or bar mitzvah is meant to thank God for no longer needing to take on the children's punishments for their misbehavior or sin.

Girls become bat mitzvah at 12, while boys become bar mitzvah at 13 in Orthodox communities. Regarding Conservative, Reconstructionist, and Reform Judaism, the children make that transition at age 13, regardless of gender. This age is when the children are expected to have an understanding of Jewish norms and ritual law, as well as ethics. They are also eligible to participate in any part of Jewish community life that they want to, the same way the grown-ups in the community do.

Teshuvah

Teshuvah means "Repentance" and is an important aspect of Judaism, for it is the atonement for sins one commits. It is known and accepted that no one is perfect and that every now and then, people will sin. However, Judaism holds that you can reduce how often you sin in the future or stop sinning altogether by repenting for the evil you've done in the past. So, the main gold of repentance in Judaism is to encourage the transformation of oneself through ethics. One who chooses to represent Judaism is a Baal teshuva, and this person is considered even more honorable than one who is righteous or has no sin.

The Talmud, a major text of Rabbinic Judaism and the foundation of halakha, states that God created repentance even before the world as we know it. It's believed that you should repent right away. There's a Talmudic parable that Rabbi Eliezer taught those who followed him: "Repent one day before your death." Clearly, being able to forecast one's death is impossible, so the followers naturally asked how they were supposed to know when they'd be passing on. In response, the Rabbi said, "All the more reason, therefore, to represent today, lest one die tomorrow." Jews believe in the Divine judgment of God and that God is always willing to accept those who repent, particularly from the start of Elul (a month) all the way to the High Holiday season (also known as the Days of Awe or the High Holy Days, also called the Yamim Noraim). These holidays include the Day of Judgment or Rosh HaShanah, the Ten Days of Repentance or Aseret Yimei Teshuva, and the Day of Atonement or Yom Kippur. The Kabbalah also includes one more holiday, known as the Hoshana Rabbah.

Repentance involves acknowledging you've sinned, choosing to forsake the path of sin, being concerned about the consequences of your sin, being humble, acting in ways opposite to the sin, confessing the sin and asking for atonement, making amends, self-restraint, and so on.

Brit

Brit is a ceremony for Jewish boys that takes place when they are eight days old. This ceremony is also known as brit shel Avraham Avinu, which means "the covenant of Abraham, our Father." It is named after Abraham, the first recipient of the circumcision mitzvah. Brit literally means "chain," "ring," or "circle," and these infer the idea of a binding covenant between God and his people. Brit is at the very center of Judaism.

The creator God entered into covenants with Abraham, Isaac, and Jacob, as well as the Israelites on Mount Sinai and the Moabite planes as they were preparing to enter Israel itself. The brit is fundamentally Jewish, and it came about when everyone was willing to let other people live their lives the way they thought fit. It developed during a time when people would negotiate existence, agreeing that not only would they be loyal to their fellow Jew, but they would also help one another. This mutual assistance ensures that everyone in the community achieves much more than they possibly could on their own. It's not something one practices only when they are in the mood, but it is a core part of being Jewish. An example of brit would be marriage, for instance. Another brit is the Brit Bein HaBetarim, also known as the Covenant of Parts. This is the covenant God made with Abraham's descendants about moving from being oppressed and enslaved strangers in a foreign land to being in their land, the Land of Canaan (Israel).

The Kabbalah and Halakhah

Halakhah comes from halakha, a root word meaning "to go." It represents the laws of Judaism, separate from the Haggadah, which is the nonlegal aspect of the religion. It's all about the relationships that you have on a personal, interpersonal, national, and international level. It's also about the different observances and practices followed by Jews. The Bible talks about what it means to live a good life, phrasing it this way: "and shalt show them the way wherein they are to go and the work that they must do." At first, the word Halakhah (plural halakhot) referred to specific laws that were given in specific situations, such as the law handed to Moses by God on Sinai (Halakhah le-Moshe mi-Sinai). This meaning still persists, but now, it does so along with the one encompassing the Jewish laws and practices.

During the rabbinic period, the study of the halakha became very important. Since it is such a difficult subject to get into and equally important for living your life as a practicing Jew, it is deemed very important to study this more than any other aspect of the Jewish religion. It is generally assumed that the halakha goes all the way back to the time of Moses, excluding the elaborations and innovations added later in line with the new situations of the newer times. The halakha is rooted in Oral Torah.

Kabbalah means "tradition," "correspondence," or "reception." It refers to a Jewish school of thought. Those who follow this school of thought are known as Mekubbal. The kabbalah's definition depends on the goals of those who follow its ways and their tradition. The Jewish Kabbalah shows followers how the eternal God who never changes is connected to the world that never stops changing, which all humans live and are a part of. It is the relationship between the Infinite — Ein Sof — and all else. If you want to understand what the Kabbalah is all about, then you have to dive deep into classical Judaism scriptures. These scriptures are rooted in a set of spiritual writings known collectively as the Zohar. Sometimes, Kabbalah is also interpreted as "occult knowledge" or "mysticism." It's about the part of Judaism that covers all things related to who God is. Kabbalists believe that God's ways are mysterious, but they also understand that one can obtain true knowledge and understanding of that which is shrouded in mystery. They believe that by obtaining this information, one can become intimate with God. Kabbalists see God and his creation as one and the same instead of considering them separate beings. They have a strong desire to connect with God.

According to the Kabbalah, a part of God is enshrined in each person's soul, waiting to come to light. Divinity is in all things that exist, and therefore there's nothing but divinity all around us. The sacred teachings of the Kabbalah are understood through investigation to discover hidden meanings, oral transmission from a master Kabbalist, or direct revelation. The latter involves spirit possession, angel visitations, and other supernatural occurrences. The Kabbalah calls on one and all to experience God in spirit and truth, not just to know about God. This task can be done through rituals meant to give followers power and through the use of this power to create changes in the physical world and the worlds beyond.

Can Anyone Follow Jewish Spirituality?

Yes, you can follow Jewish spirituality. Just because practitioners don't try to convert people, you'll find that Judaism is open to one and all today. Conversion makes you as much a Jew as those who were born to Jewish mothers. The Biblical Ruth isn't just King David's great-great-grandmother but was also a convert to Judaism. The thing about conversions is that they tend to be accepted based on the Jewish community in question. For the most part, Orthodox Jews are very strict about where and how conversions are carried out and hardly endorse liberal Jewish conversions. Orthodox Jews may not accept your conversion as valid if it's done by a non-Orthodox institution because, for the most part, they don't consider non-Orthodox rabbis as actual rabbis. However, this shouldn't stop you from wanting to convert to Judaism and doing so.

Chapter Two: Sacred Jewish Symbols

This chapter will teach you about the most important Jewish symbols, their meaning, and why they matter. These symbols have some history. Some of them are more for religious practice, while others are more spiritual and cultural in nature.

The Menorah

The menorah is the representation of universal enlightenment and Talmudic wisdom. This candelabra has seven lamps, representing all seven branches of human knowledge. Six lamps bend inwards and are guided by the middle lamp, representing God's light. The menorah also represents that creation took place in seven days, and the middle lamp represents the Sabbath, on which no work takes place, and no sin is committed.

The Menorah.

While the previous menorah is known as the Talmudic menorah, the Hanukkah menorah has nine branches, not seven. A fascinating thing happened when the Jewish Temple was destroyed by the West Asian Seleucid Empire. You see, the lams in the Temple had to be lit by specially prepared olive oil that was consecrated for that purpose only. However, much of it was destroyed, leaving only enough for the eternal flame to burn for a day and no more. So there was simply no hope that the flame wouldn't die out. However, a miracle happened. Day after day, the flame continued to burn with the reserved oil, and it was only used up by the eighth day, at which time there was now fresh oil to keep the flame burning. According to the Talmud, the seven-flamed menorah must only be used within the Temple walls.

The Dreidel

The Dreidel.

The dreidel is also known as the dreidl or dreidle. It's a spinning top with four sides, often played during Hanukkah. It's like the Jewish version of the European teetotum, a gambling toy. All four faces of the dreidel have a Hebrew letter on them. The letters are:

- Nun
- Gimel
- Hei
- Shin

Nun means "nothing," gimel means "whole," hei means "half," and shin means "put in." Etymologically speaking, these letters stand in for the phrase "nes gadol haya sham," or "a great miracle happened there." This is about the Miracle of Hanukkah, where the oil lasted longer than was expected. There's a different phrase that is used, which is "nes gadol haya po," (which has the same meaning as the previous phrase except for the word "there" is replaced with "here." Because of this phrase, it's more common to find dreidels with pe inscribed on them rather than shin. However, those in the Haredi communities say shin is the right letter for the Holy Land, as "there" refers to the Holy Temple itself. The dreidel is the game traditionally played during Hanukkah.

The Torah

Judaism is founded on the Torah, which represents the rabbinical teachings and law you're meant to follow as a Jew. Moses received the Torah from God himself to share with the people on Mount Sinai, and this collection of five books is considered one of Judaism's holiest items. A Torah scribe or Sefer writes the scroll using a certain parchment paper, which is then put into the ark (the Aron ha Kodesh), a sacred storage space. Writing the scrolls can take a year and a half to finish, as this involves preparing the animal skins to be used, as well as writing the scroll without making any mistakes. Mistakes make the scroll invalid or *pasul*. When the scroll is complete, it's called a Sefer Torah.

The Sefer Torah is a sacred scroll not just because it's the core of Judaism but because if you accidentally drop it in the synagogue, everyone present would have no choice but to fast for 40 days. Whenever the Jewish people had trouble and persecution, much effort would go into keeping the scrolls safe from harm because the Torah matters that much to them.

Every week, Jewish people gather to read the Torah as part of the activities during Shabbat services. These are the five alternative names for each book of the Torah, also called the Chameesha Choomshey Torah:

- Bresheit (Genesis)
- Shemot (Exodus)
- Vayicra (Leviticus)
- Bamidbar (Numbers)
- Devarim (Deuteronomy)

Moses received the Torah precisely 50 days after the Jews had left Egypt. The Torah describes the way God wants his people to live and express themselves, and it has 613 commandments for the people to follow. Ten of those are known as the Ten Commandments. These commandments are all written in Hebrew, the oldest Jewish language. The books are also known as the Law of Moses or Torat Moshe.

The entire scroll of the Torah is read in order over an entire year, starting from the end of the autumn celebration known as Sukkot. The aspects of the Torah that are read are known as the parshioth. There are usually anywhere from three to five chapters. Reading from the scroll is no mean feat because you need to be able to read the letters without needing the matching vowels. This means you've got to know the portion you're reading so well that you make no mistakes. The reading is more in the form of a song, and the tune it's sung to is rather ancient.

The scrolls are unfurled and set on a raised platform in the synagogue's center. This platform is known as the Bimah. No one touches the scrolls directly, as they use a pointer called a Yad instead. The Yad resembles a hand with a finger pointing out. The chanting must be done by someone trained specifically for this purpose, but the rabbi could also do it instead. If you're ever asked to join the congregation or witness a Shabbat reading, you should appreciate it because it's no mean thing. You're going to take part in an Aliyah, which is a word that means "going up."

The Tallit

When you're saying prayers, you'll have to use the tallit, which is a special prayer shawl. The shawl often has four corners, and it covers your shoulders. According to the Torah, all Jews have to do mitzvahs wearing a tallit with tzitzit, which are the knotted fringes on each corner of the shawl. The fringes, while beautiful, are more than just for aesthetic purposes. They are a reminder about the necessity of following the word of God, making no exemptions in the process. The cloth part is known as the begged, often made from cotton or wool and, now and then, from silk. Before putting the tallit on, you must say a certain blessing first. Some Jewish communities do not allow anyone to put it on unless or until it's their Bat or Bar Mitzvah. Other communities only whip out the tallit during the marriage.

The Tallit.
https://www.pexels.com/photo/a-person-in-a-tallit-reading-a-chumash-5974346/

There's no specific commandment in the Bible about having to put on a Tallit because the assumption during those times was that the people would have some sort of garment on to keep themselves covered anyway. The instruction given to the Israelites was that they had to attach the tzitzit to the corners of their garments, as indicated in Deuteronomy Chapter 22, verse 12.

The Kippah or Yarmulke

The Kippah.
https://www.pexels.com/photo/boy-lighting-menorah-3730985/

The Yarmulke is a small head covering that's round. It's worn by the Jews. The word Yarmulke is Yiddish, while Kippah is Hebrew. The purpose of this small hat is to remind the practitioner that no matter what, there's always someone who stands above you. The males of the Orthodox Judaism community always have their Kippah on, no matter what. Who wears a yarmulke, and when? Some Jewish sects will put them on only during religious ceremonies and services. Traditionally, all women are expected to keep their heads covered, particularly with the non-Orthodox Jewish denominations. You can expect the yarmulke to be offered as a gift during Bar and Bat Mitzvah occasions, and the recipient is expected to keep it on the entire time.

The Siddur

The Siddur.
Brian Jeffery Beggerly, CC BY 2.0 <https://creativecommons.org/licenses/by/2.0>, via Wikimedia Commons https://commons.wikimedia.org/wiki/File:A_Siddur.jpg

The Siddur is a Jewish prayer book that contains Jewish liturgical texts. Siddur is "order" in Hebrew. The foundation of Siddur is the Prophets' prayers and the Torah. Note that not every prayer in the Siddur was there from the first versions, as some newer ones were incorporated over time. You may find all sorts of versions of Siddur, with some having prayers specifically for synagogue services held during the week, while others have prayers that cover Shabbat as well. You can also find Sukkot, Shavuot, and Passover prayers in the Siddur, which differs from one denomination to another.

The Mezuzah

The Mezuzah.

The mezuzah is kept at the doorpost. You can find the roots of the mezuzah in the Book of Deuteronomy, specifically in the portion where God told the Israelites they had to ensure they lived by his commandments and never forgot anything he told them. How? They were expected to write God's words on the doorposts of their homes. This special case has a scroll in it that has the words of Shema, and the outside of the container has Shin etched into it. If you're going to hang it up in your home, do so at an angle, and keep in mind you're not to allow people to fiddle with it because it's not just something for decoration but is a sacred object to be respected.

The Yad

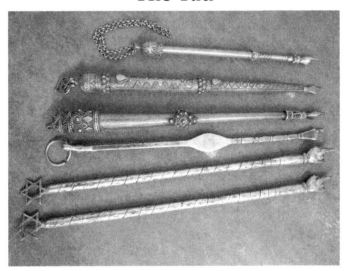

The Yad.
Chennaidl, CC BY-SA 4.0 <https://creativecommons.org/licenses/by-sa/4.0>, via Wikimedia Commons https://commons.wikimedia.org/wiki/File:Silver_Yad.jpg

The Yad tends to be used just as decoration, but when it's functional, it serves as a pointer. Rather than use your hand to read the Torah, you use the Yad instead so you can hold your place as the Torah is read in the synagogue or as it's sung. The Yad acts as your hand, and small wonder it does, since the word itself means "hand." It helps you to keep your place without soiling the Torah with your bare hands.

The Challah

The Challah.

This is a special kind of bread that Jewish people eat. It is golden brown, and the dough is twisted. This bread goes back to when the Israelites left Egypt and wandered about in the desert for 40 years. According to the Torah, the manna fell from the sky as they journeyed. This manna was like bread, and it helped sustain the Israelites. Now, Jews practice baking the challah, a sweet bread made with yeast and eggs and braided to form different shapes. Some bakers put a modern spin on things by adding chocolate chips or raisins. It's a lovely loaf to have but also of deep spiritual importance. During Rosh Hashanah, expect to be served challah that is round, but don't just eat it without knowing its significance. The circular shape is a reminder that life is a circle and a cycle. You might notice your challah loaf has 12 bumps on it. This is no coincidence, as each one represents an Israelite tribe. Here they are in order of birth:

- Reuben
- Simeon
- Levi
- Judah

- Issachar
- Zebulun
- Dan
- Naphtali
- Gad
- Asher
- Benjamin
- Joseph

Pomegranate

Pomegranate is a delicious fruit that has deep meaning in Judaism. It's meant to act as a reminder of the idea of love and the blessings of God that cause his people to be fertile in all their ways. Reading through the Book of Solomon, also known as the Song of Songs, you'll find the pomegranate makes frequent appearances. You should also know that even the seeds of this fruit are important, as they are a representation of the mitzvot which you must follow. Each of the 613 seeds in a pomegranate represents the mitzvot's 613 commandments. On Rosh Hashanah, this fruit is often served to make the new year one that is prosperous and wonderful for one and all.

The Shofar

The Shofar.

Jonathunder, CC BY-SA 3.0 <https://creativecommons.org/licenses/by-sa/3.0>, via Wikimedia Commons https://commons.wikimedia.org/wiki/File:ShofarSound.JPG

The shofar is a unique item. This is no ordinary horn, as there are specific times and events during which it is blown. If it's not Rosh Hashanah or Yom Kippur, don't expect to hear the shofar. Another time when it's often blown is in Elui, a Jewish month. The mitzvah commands that you must listen to the blast of the shofar during these specific times, and not only that, the shofar is meant to blast the teruah, shevarim, and tekiah. You can get this horn in all sizes and shapes, and children and adults are welcome to blast them as they like.

The Kiddush Cup

The Kiddush Cup.
Ivorymammoth at the English Wikipedia, CC BY-SA 3.0
<http://creativecommons.org/licenses/by-sa/3.0/>, via Wikimedia Commons
https://commons.wikimedia.org/wiki/File:Kiddush_cup_jerusalem.jpg

This is a beautiful goblet made of silver, used for sacred drinks. This is one of the more common symbols in Judaism, and the word Kiddush translates to "sanctification." During the Passover seder or at a table specially prepared for Shabbat, you can expect to see the Kiddush make an appearance. It's used to bless the drink it carries, and when Shabbat officially comes to an end, you'll observe the standard practice is to begin Havdalah. Don't be too shocked if you notice someone continues to pour wine or grape juice into the Kiddush despite the fact that it's already flowing over. That's meant to represent the way God blesses his people, richly and abundantly, with no limit. This practice is a sign and a reminder that blessings are abundant for the coming week. This cup is also presented to a Bat or Bar Mitzvah as a gift.

Tefillin

Tefflin.

These are two black boxes made of leather. They are small and are usually bound to your forehead and just above your bicep. The Torah does not mention the tefillin, but the practice of placing the word of God on your arm and between both eyes is something the Torah talks about at least four times twice when the Israelites had to flee Egypt to go to the land promised to them by God, and twice more in the sacred Shema. You'll have these items bound to your arm and head, strapped securely in place, often with leather. It's standard practice to lay out the Tefillin when you pray early in the morning during the week, as this is what God wants.

The Chai

Chai is Hebrew for "life," and it's worn as an adornment on your neck. The word has the letters Chet and Yud. Chet happens to be the 8th Hebrew letter, and Yid is the 10th. Putting them together means you get the numerological value of 18, which is why the number 18 matters deeply in Judaism. Giving money to a Bat or Bar Mitzvah, a wedding, or even to charity is a practice to give in multiples of 18, as this represents the idea of giving life itself.

The Grogger

Every Jew knows the importance of recounting the story of Haman, who was an evil character in the Bible that was bent on the eradication of the Jews, much like several other people have been in Jewish history. When recounting this story, it's important to have the grogger present. The retelling is done during Purim, and it's important because it helps you remember how close Jews came to being annihilated and how God stepped in to save the people from Haman. You're obligated by law to hear the Purim story, which is what the Megillah is centered on. Each time Haman's name comes up, you take your grogger and give it a spin while booing him. The sound is reminiscent of grinding metal.

The Ten Commandments

All Jewish law is founded upon the ten commandments. They are depicted as large stone tablets with the commandments carved on them. They are commandments for how people should relate with God and how they should relate with other humans. The commandment that asks the faithful to honor their father and more is the connection between both relationships. There's a holiday known as the Shavuot, which happens in Spring. This holiday is meant to honor the receiving of the ten commandments by the Jewish people.

The Hamsa

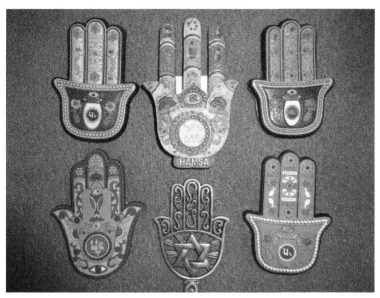

The Hamsa.

This symbol resembles a palm and is used not just by the Jews but by other religions as well. Usually worn as an amulet, you can put it on to keep yourself from becoming a victim of the evil eye. Hamsa is God's hand, shielding you from the deluge of your enemies and their ill intentions and machinations toward you, and that is why many Jews put on this amulet. Some people only think of it as a fashion piece, but they are missing out on its power by staying ignorant of what it's really about and how it can help them.

The Lulav and Etrog

A common Sukkot practice is to get four plants, myrtle, palm, willow, and etrog, and string them up together. These four plants then form something called the lulav. They wave this lulav in all directions to represent the idea that the Jewish people are one and to remind themselves of God's omnipresence. The standard practice is to shake the lulav while holding the etrog, and you must do this with deep reverence. When you want to buy the etrog, note that it's got to be in a velvet box.

This way, the fruit (which is like a lemon) stays kosher, and the stem isn't destroyed.

The Magen David

The Magen David is also known as the Star of David and has six points. You may have seen this symbol on Israel's flag as a blue star against a white area, with blue frames surrounding the star. The symbol is said to be from the 1600s, and the Jewish people in Prague were the first to use the Magen David as their official symbol. After that, the symbol became popular all through Eastern Europe. By 1897, those who would go on to found Israel decided the Magen David would be the representation of Zionism, and this happened at the First Zionist Congress.

The Ketubah

The Ketubah must be signed by spouses who intend to get married to each other. It's a Jewish contract that regulates marriage based on Jewish law. Those who are to be wed must sign the contract first, and there have to be others present to act as witnesses to the process. You cannot get this signed if there isn't a rabbit to officiate and validate the document, which is a unique one, to say the least. Rather than a boring legal document, this one talks about the hopes and dreams of the happy couple through stunning artwork. The art could be done through any medium, from watercolor to oils and so on. Usually, the focal point of the art is the couple's home.

The Tree of Life

This is also known as Etz Chaim in Hebrew. It's meant to act as a metaphor, representing the Torah. The meaning of this symbol goes far back to the time of Eden when God created a garden full of wonderful trees. Among those trees were the tree of knowledge of good and evil and the tree of life. You'll find the Etz Chaim in most Jewish buildings and art, and many synagogues will work with the tree into their designs.

The Havdalah Set

Havdalah is a ritual meant to act as a separator between Shabbat and the other ceremonies of the week. The Shabbat has to be ended properly; a special day of rest held each week. Havdalah is that ending. During Havdalah, the Jews will say blessings over a cup full of wine, lovely-smelling spices, and a flame. Before the blessing, there has to be a clear sky at night so that three specific stars are visible to one and all. There are certain items required for you to celebrate the event of Havdalah, among them being a special tray, a braided candle, a box of spices, and the silver Kiddush. Everyone huddles together in the dark, forming a circle, and then blessings are sung while people pass the spices around to smell them. The spices are usually cloves, cinnamon, and cardamom. The wine from the Kiddush is poured over the candle's flame, marking the end of Shabbat.

Candles

Candles are a part of most Jewish rituals and holidays. When performing Shabbat, blessings are recited over candles. Traditionally, it's the matriarch who gets to light candles for Shabbat. When she's done, she must wave her hands around the flames thrice, working with a circular motion. This wave isn't random but is meant to bless the fires as they burn. These days, anyone other than the female head of the home can do this. If you could peek in on a Jewish family, you'll notice they have two candles meant to stand in for Shabbat's two obligations. These candles are intricately designed, and they stay in the family for generations. Sometimes they could be made of silver or clay.

The Seder Plate

Usually, these plates have separate parts for each item needed for the seder. The items are:

- **Parsley dipped in salt water:** This is a symbol of how much the people wept during their time with the Egyptians as their slave masters.

- **Charoset:** This is meant to be a representation of the mortar that the Israelites had to work with day in and day out while making bricks to build the Egyptian empire.

- **Horseradish or other bitter herbs:** This reminds the people of how terrible it was to be enslaved, to have one's free will taken from them, and be forced into a cruel, bitter life.

- **Lettuce or other greens:** This is yet another representation of the brutality of the enslaved way of living and how it completely breaks the soul.

- **A shank bone:** This is the sacrifice of the Israelites.

- **A roasted egg:** This represents the cycles of life and death.

The larger the feast, the more seder plates will be made available for every attendant to look upon and remember what their ancestors had to go through at the hands of their oppressors.

Chapter Three: The Sefirot and Ein Sof

The Sefirot are important aspects of the Kabbalah and represent the ten emanations through which the Ein Sof (or God) reveals his mysteries. Before diving into the Ein Sof and the Sefirot, here's a little more about the Kabbalah.

Kabbalah

When one lives by the Kabbalah, they are known as a Mekubbal. The Kabbalah's entire purpose is to make clear the connection between Ein Sof and his creation, making up the basis of Judaism, its beliefs, and practices. At first, the Jewish Kabbalists passed on their sacred texts within Judaism and would turn to the scriptures to shed light on the mystical knowledge they sought.

For traditional Kabbalists, the origins of the Kabbalah are from before the other religions in the world were a thing. They believe that the Kabbalah is the foundation of the politics, arts, sciences, religions, and world views that exist right now. Kabbalah comes from the earliest days of Jewish mysticism, and reinterpretations began during the 16th century in Ottoman Palestine. The Zohar is also important to the Kabbalah, which draws most of its meaning from there. Those who follow Kabbalah believe that studying this path and the Torah is important.

These are the foundational views of the Kabbalah:

1. There are ten aspects of God, and it is through these aspects that everything in life was created.

2. The Kabbalah's light of wisdom was given to the angels and Adam, Abraham, and Moses.

3. The human soul exists and has always existed before incarnating on Earth.

4. The soul reincarnates.

5. There are higher realms of existence or consciousness.

6. There are multiple universes.

7. Consciousness is connected at every level, from angels and demons to thought forms and incarnations.

8. Michael, Gabriel, Raphael, and Uriel are the four archangels, and they play powerful roles in the faith. Then there's Sandalphon, who, like Michael, is an angel of prayer. There's also Liliel, the Angel of the Night, and Lilith, the female devil.

9. Two Messiahs exist. One is of Joseph's bloodline, and the other is of David's.

10. Adam and Eve fell from grace because they couldn't make a correction that would move existence to a higher level of consciousness.

11. You can directly experience God and don't need to have Jesus or anyone else mediate on your behalf.

The Sefirot

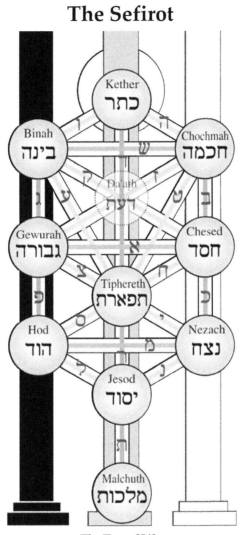

The Tree of Life.

The Tree of Life is central to the Kabbalah. It's a sacred symbol that shows the ten Sephirot or Sefirot, which are the different aspects or revelations of the Creator. It's a spiritual light that shows the true nature of the Ein Sof. The singular form of the Sefirot is Sefirah or Sephirah. All ten of these aspects have the laws that govern all creation, including the things which were, are, and will be. The Tree of Life in Kabbalah is a model for all creation and man. The Tree of Life grows outwards from the Creator's divinity (Ein Sof, who has no end), being beyond the Sefirot themselves, as well as physical existence (that which comes from and is subordinate to the Sefirot). These are the ten Sefirot. It's important to note that they can be spelled differently:

- Keter or Kether(Crown)
- Hochmah or Chochmah(Wisdom)
- Binah (Understanding)
- Gevurah or Gewurah(Judgment)
- Hesed or Chesed(Kindness)
- Tiphereth (Beauty)
- Hod (Splendor)
- Netzah or Nezach(Eternity)
- Yesod or Jesod (Foundation)
- Malkhut or Malchuth (Kingdom)

Keter is the divine will of Ein Sof, the Creator, and the Sefirah, above all the others on the Kabbalistic Tree of Life. Just as the crown goes on the head, encircling it, the Keter contains all the other Sefirot. This Sefirah sits in a position that can't easily be unpacked and understood by the human mind, and for this reason, it's also known as "the most hidden of all hidden things." Alternatively, you may hear it referred to as Ayin, which means "nothing." Ayin represents the idea that the crown's secrets are so buried in mysteries that no one could try to deduce its true meaning or understand it through contemplation, debate, or any other means. Keter is the embodiment of compassion as well, as the Creator is the perfection in its final form, and Keter, being close to the Creator, has no flaws.

Hochmah is also known as Chochmah. It is the epitome of wisdom. This Sefirah is the Supernal Mind and the Oneness of all things. It's God's first act of creation, the beginning from which all things sprung. In the Kabbalah, wisdom is no ordinary thing. The undifferentiated mind isn't yet broken down by the thinking process. Consider it the first brilliant flash of an idea, whole and indivisible, before you begin breaking it down into its components, other ideas, and concepts. It is inspiration beyond division, where everything exists as one thing, which is the attribute of life not confined by space, time, or definitions. It's the unmanifested potential of all life.

Binah is understanding. Where Chochmah is undifferentiated inspiration, Binah is the separation of that mind or inspiration. It is the breakdown of the One into its many details, making it comprehensible for one and all. This is the level where ideas can exist on their own, on a level that makes it easy for anyone to examine them. This Sefirah is where everyone's soul comes from, and it is all about breaking things down into individual, distinct components. Binah is, therefore, the process of fleshing out the abstract into something more concrete.

Da'at is knowledge. This isn't exactly a Sefirah, but it serves as the connection between Chochmah (wisdom) and Binah (understanding). However, since it plays a very important role in this way, it acts like a legit Sefirah. This is why some systems like the Arizal will include Da'at in the Keter's place as the tenth Sefirah. Da'at is the invisible space between the Sefirot, and for Keter's energy to flow down to the other Sefirot, this space has to be crossed. Consider the process of creating something. At the start of the creation process, there's a crucial step: formulation of an idea. However, there's a chance that there's no will to flesh out that idea, or the will won't be enough to see the idea through to completion. Da'at is, therefore, like the will required to bring things that start to a finish, and you can think of it as an eleventh Sefirah, albeit hidden and parallel to Tiferet.

Hesed is also known as Chesed and is Kindness. It refers to the process of expansion and the concept of benevolence with no limits regarding God. God's benevolence is beyond benevolent, being the essence of abundance. It's about the divine quality of God that continues to expand without bounds. All souls can recognize this abundance, and they desire to be open to all things created, so they can express their goodness to it in the same way God expresses goodness to one and all.

Gevurah represents judgment, law, strength, and the limits of expansion. While Chesed represents expansion, Gevurah is contraction. Chesed allows energy to flow freely, while Gevurah acts as a means to limit and control the flow, acting as a counterbalance to Chesed. Both of these Sefirot are balanced out by the Tiferet. Gevurah is the expression of restraint, discernment, and judgment. The reason Gevurah is necessary is that there has to be justice in the way that Chesed is shared among all. The universe operates on a merit system; therefore, you get the kindness you deserve. Gevurah is also essential for encouraging progress, action, and purpose. Its power and force are the requirements you must have to act on your desire for expansion, despite the obstacles you may encounter in the process.

Tiferet is also known as Tiphareth or Tiferet. The Sefirah lies in the middle of the Tree of Life and embodies the essence of truth and beauty. Tiferet acts as a balancing force for the entire Tree of Life, as, other than Malkhut, each Sefirah must flow into Tiferet. It represents the connection between heaven and Earth, which is depicted by the straight line that leads from Keter to Malchut. This Sefirah is on the Tree's middle column, which gives the other aspects balance, harmony in their functions, and a seamless synthesis of Chesed's outflow and Gevurah's restriction. You'll notice that the Tiferet is somewhat closer to Chesed. This proximity is why the Tiferet is known as Rachamim, compassion or mercy. It's also the aspect that is known for beauty, especially in the way it balances all the Sefirot.

Netzah is also called Netzach, and the Sefirah represents the concept of endless cycles and eternity. It also represents victory. This one is an extension of the power of Chesed. Netzach is the power that overcomes all obstacles in the way of the benevolence of God flowing to those meant to receive it. This is eternity itself, meaning that there are cycles that repeat endlessly, and they have no choice but to continue to keep all of creation in balance and stability.

Hod is the extension of Gevurah, representing the ideas of splendor and glory. This Sefirah is all about responsiveness. Where Netzach is all about the outpouring of all that is good, Hod is there to keep that benevolence in check. This way, it's impossible for God's benevolence to reach those who do not deserve it, and as a result, God continues to reign in his splendor and glory.

Yesod is the foundation. It acts as the connection between He who gives and they who receive. It is the unity between all other Sefirot and Malkhut. Yesod receives light from all the other Sefirot, synthesizes the light, and channels it as needed. This way, the emanations of the other aspects can flow to that which is created.

Malchut is also called Malkhut. It represents the Kingdom of the Divine and is why the physical world exists. This last Sefirah is distinct from the others because it doesn't have its own light. Instead, Malkhut receives light from the other aspects of the Tree of Life. Think of it like the moon, which only reflects sunlight and has no light of its own. Malkhut is the Sefirah that brings all things into existence in this lower, physical realm. Everything that has ever been is contained in this aspect, and its energy is dense and constricted. The world you can see around you is connected to Malkhut, representing the mouth and the power of the divine word of God. Malkhut also steadily interacts with Binah, as that which is abstract is made concrete in this created, physical world.

The Concept of Oneness

When you think of the Sefirot of the Tree of Life in Kabbalah, you should think of them as lights for your spiritual path. They are also responsible for all manifestations, showing the different aspects of Ein Sof. It's the same way a person can have different qualities, like loyalty, bravery, etc. Remember that the different Sefirot are not different gods, as only one God exists. They are simply different aspects of the same Creator, and one must never assume that there's duality in him.

The Oneness of the Divine is at the heart of Kabbalah. All followers must keep this in mind regardless of the circumstances. The Creator has no limits, which may be hard to comprehend from a limited human point of view. So the best thing we have are the Sephirot, which helps us to understand the limited aspects of the unlimited God.

Three Pillars, One Tree

Note that the Tree of Life has three pillars on the right, left, and middle. The pillar on the right represents expansion, the one on the left is constriction, and the middle acts as a balance between the other two pillars. These lines are meant to act as pillars of the faith working together as a synergistic whole. The pillars are Kindness (necessary as a reward for living righteously), Judgment (required to ensure balance and restitution to those who have been wronged or those who should get their just deserts for their choices), and Mercy (which makes it possible for one and all to be forgiven and brought back into the loving grace of Ein Sof). The right pillar is masculine, all about action. It is the giver.

There's also the pillar on the left, which is more about receiving and being passive, both of which are feminine qualities. Finally, the pillar in the middle connects the other two and brings balance to these energies so that they manifest as they should.

Sephirothic Correspondences

The correspondences of the Sefirot refer to symbols, qualities, and other associations that can help you understand what each Sefirah stands for. Below are the correspondences of the Sefirot. Note that some of the planets here aren't actual planets. The element refers to the physical, classical elements that match the Sefirah's nature. Also, there's the Briatic correspondence, an abstract quality that captures the essence of the Sefirah's expression. The illusion refers to how the Sefirah's energy can cause us not to judge things clearly, showing up as "obvious truths," while the obligation is what you need to express at that level. Virtue and Vice are the Sefirah's energy manifesting for better or worse in your personality. You'll also see the corresponding Qliphoth (more on that later), spiritual experience, the name of God used to invoke the Sefirah's power, and more.

Keter

Meaning: Crown

Color: Pure white

Number: 1

Spiritual Experience: Union with God

Archangel: Metatron

Angel Order: Chaioth ha Qadesh

Name of God: Eheieh

Qliphoth: Futility

Planet: Rashith ha Gilgalim

Briatic Correspondence: Unity

Illusion: Attainment

Virtue: Attainment

Vice: Nil

Alternative Names: the Greater Countenance (Macroprosopus), the Smooth Point, Concealed of the Concealed, Rum Maalah, the Highest Point, Existence of Existences, Ancient of Days

Keywords: God, unity, pure consciousness, union, the Godhead, emanation, source, manifestation.

Chokhmah

Meaning: Wisdom

Color: Gray, silver, or white

Number: 2

Spiritual Experience: Face-to-face vision of God

Archangel: Raziel

Angel Order: Auphanim

Name of God: Jah

Qliphoth: Arbitrariness

Planet: Mazlot

Briatic Correspondence: Revolution

Illusion: Independence

Virtue: Good

Vice: Evil

Alternative Names: The Supernal Father, Abba, the Father.

Keywords: The wellspring, lifeforce, pure creative energy

Binah

Meaning: Understanding

Color: Black

Number: 3

Spiritual Experience: Vision of Sorrow

Archangel: Cassiel

Angel Order: Aralim

Name of God: Elohim

Qliphoth: Fatalism

Planet: Shabbathai (or Saturn)

Briatic Correspondence: Comprehension

Illusion: Death

Virtue: Silence

Vice: Inertia

Alternative Names: Ama, Marah, Aima, Khorsia, the Throne, the Crone, the Mother, the Superior Mother, the Mother of Form, Intelligence, the Fifty Gates of Understanding.

Keywords: Constraint, slowness, limits, karma, infertility, old age, time, fate, the womb and gestation, natural law, space, death, weaving and spinning, fertility, containment, boundedness, annihilation, enclosure, mother.

Chesed

Meaning: Mercy

Color: Blue

Number: 4

Spiritual Experience: Vision of Love

Archangel: Zadkiel

Angel Order: Chasmalim

Name of God: El

Qliphoth: Ideology

Planet: Tzadekh (or Jupiter)

Briatic Correspondence: Authority

Illusion: Self-righteousness (or being right)

Virtue: Humility

Vice: Gluttony, hypocrisy, bigotry, tyranny

Obligation: Humility, obedience

Alternative Names: Majesty, love, magnificence, Gedulah.

Keywords: Secular power, spiritual power, creativity, vision, inspiration, authority, leadership, submission, waste, excess, the atom bomb, service, birth, obliteration, the Annihilation Myth.

Gevurah

Meaning: Strength

Color: Red

Number: 5

Spiritual Experience: Vision of Power

Archangel: Camael

Angel Order: Seraphim

Name of God: Elohim Gevor

Qliphoth: Bureaucracy

Planet: Madim (or Mars)

Briatic Correspondence: Power

Illusion: Invincibility

Virtue: Energy, courage

Vice: Cruelty

Obligation: Loyalty, courage

Alternative Names: Justice, Din, fear, Pachad

Keywords: Cold retribution, executed law, power, cruelty, justice, domination, oppression, the Power Myth, catabolism, needed destruction, martial arts.

Tifereth

Meaning: Beauty

Color: Yellow

Number: 6

Element: Fire

Spiritual Experience: Vision of Harmony

Archangel: Michael

Angel Order: Malachim

Name of God: Aloah va Daath

Qliphoth: Hollowness

Planet: Shemesh (or the Sun)

Briatic Correspondence: Wholeness, centrality
Illusion: Identification
Virtue: Devotion to the Great Work
Vice: Self-importance, pride
Obligation: Integrity
Command: Dare
Alternative Names: The Microprosopus, the King, Melekh, the Son, Zoar Anpin, Rachamin, charity.

Keywords: Wholeness, balance, identity, integrity, self-importance, harmony, centrality, self-sacrifice, the Philosopher's Stone, the Self, the Son of God, the solar plexus, the Great Work, the King.

Netzach

Meaning: Firmness, victory
Color: Green
Number: 7
Element: Water
Spiritual Experience: Vision of Beauty Triumphant
Archangel: Haniel
Angel Order: Elohim
Name of God: Jehovah Tzabaoth
Qliphoth: Routine, habit
Planet: Nogah (or Venus)
Briatic Correspondence: Nurture
Illusion: Projection
Virtue: Unselfishness
Vice: Selfishness
Obligation: Responsibility
Command: Know

Keywords: Emotions, drives, sensual beauty, feelings, luxury, pleasure, passion, libido, nurture, ecstasy, sympathy, empathy.

Hod

Meaning: Splendor, glory
Color: Orange
Number: 8
Element: Air
Spiritual Experience: Vision of Splendor
Archangel: Raphael
Angel Order: Beni Elohim
Name of God: Elohim Tzabaoth
Qliphoth: Rigidity
Planet: Kokab (or Mercury)
Briatic Correspondence: Abstraction
Illusion: Order
Virtue: Truth, honesty
Vice: Dishonesty
Obligation: Learn
Command: Will

Keywords: Language, the sciences, communication, reason, logic, abstraction, conceptualization, the concept of money, speech, media communication, trickery, healing, medicine, writing, philosophy, protocol, pedantry, the abstract Kabbalah system, the Law, rights, theft, territory, ownership.

Yesod

Meaning: Foundation
Color: Purple
Number: 9
Element: Aethyr (or ether)
Spiritual Experience: Vision of the Machinery of the Universe
Archangel: Gabriel
Angel Order: Cherubim
Name of God: Shaddai el Chai

Qliphoth: Robotism, zombieism

Planet: Levanah (or the Moon)

Briatic Correspondence: Perception, receptivity

Illusion: Security

Virtue: Independence

Vice: Idleness

Obligation: Trust

Command: Go

Alternative Names: The Treasure House of Images

Keywords: Imagination, interface, appearance, perception, image, the noon, glamor, instinct, hidden infrastructure, the unconscious, dreams, illusion, divination, tides, things as they seem to be and not as they are in reality, crystals, mirrors, sex, reproduction, genitals, glue, tunnels, the astral realm, aethyr, cosmetics, secret doors, instinctive magic or psychism, shamanic tunnels.

Malkuth

Meaning: Kingdom

Color: Brown (or black, olive green, russet red, citrine)

Number: 10

Element: Earth

Spiritual Experience: Vision of the Holy Guardian Angel

Archangel: Sandalphon

Angel Order: Ishim

Name of God: Adonai Malekh, Adonai ha Aretz

Qliphoth: Stasis

Planet: Cholem Yesodeth (or Earth, the sphere of the elements, the Breaker of the Foundations)

Briatic Correspondence: Stability

Illusion: Materialism

Virtue: Discrimination

Vice: Inertia, avarice

Obligation: Discipline

Command: Silence

Alternative Names: The Inferior Mother, the Gate, the Queen, Malkah, the Gate of Tears, Kallah, the Bride, the Gate of Death, the Virgin.

Keywords: Mother Earth, the Earth, the natural world, the physical elements, physical matter, sticks and stones, possessions, incarnation, feces, inertia, stability, solidity, practicality, heaviness, death of the body.

On Ein Sof

Ein Sof is the Divine God. It is the Infinite God who has no humanly discernible form. Those who follow the Kabbalistic path understand that God and his creation continue to evolve together and are the embodiment of different qualities and stages. The later stages are not just opposed to the earlier ones but also encompass them. Ein Sof is equal parts as simple as complex a being. It is everything and nothing at the same time, the embodiment of what is revealed and that remains secret. Ein Sof contains and expresses illusion and reality, being a human creation and creating humans simultaneously. As Ein Sof continues to evolve and expand, what can be gleaned from its revelation is that it is nothing or Ayin, as well as the totality of existence and the Infinite Will called Ratzon. Ein Sof represents wisdom, thought, and all things considered valuable and important (expressed through the Sefirot).

Ein Sof is the unity of the masculine and the feminine. If you've followed so far, it embodies every possible contradiction. The nature of Ein Sof implies that it is always in the process of redefining and recreating itself. One way this recreation manifests itself is in human creativity, where everyone works with hands, minds, and spirits to save a world full of chaos and contradiction.

There are various terms that Kabbalists use to refer to the hidden God, like "the concealed light," "that which thought cannot contain," "the concealment of secrecy," and so on. These terms express clearly that Ein Sof cannot be known in full. However, there are other terms like "Great Reality," "Indifferent Unity," "Root of all roots," "Prime Mover," "Cause of Causes," and so on that make it clear that Ein Sof is where everything that exists begins, as well as the combination of all things. The Sefer Yetzirah says this about Ein Sof: "Restrain your mouth from speaking and your heart from thinking, and if your heart runs, let it return to its place."

If you've ever wondered why anything exists and what the purpose of humanity is, the answer lies in Ein Sof. Being the source of all value and meaning, known and unknown, Ein Sof created the world so he could understand himself. The values of Ein Sof were originally in abstract form, and the only way to know them was to have them made real or concrete in humanity. Ein Sof contains and is both being and nothingness, but Ein Sof cannot be complete unless and until he becomes real — a process that happens through mankind's spiritual activities. Ein Sof's reflection can be seen in the human heart, soul, and deeds. If you'd like to learn more about the Sefirot and Ein Sof, look at the Sefer Yetzirah and study it.

The Qliphoth

The Qliphoth are the polar opposite of the Sefirot. Also known as the Klippot (singular, Qliphah), they represent evil in the Kabbalah. The word Kippot is Hebrew for "peels." The reason they are known as peels is that they are nothing but empty husks that used to contain the spark of divinity, and they were cast down from heaven after Adam and Even had gone against the commandment of God to not eat of the Tree of Knowledge of Good and Evil in the Eden, as is recorded in Genesis. The Qliphoth can appear in different forms, from road accidents to natural disasters, demons, and other mythical creatures.

Just as there are ten emanations or enumerations of the Divine, there are ten Qliphoth manifestations or emanations of darkness. This darkness cannot receive the light of God. You may think of the Qliphoth as the attributes of a condition against God. They act as the answer to the age-old question, "If there's a God and he's all-powerful, how and why does evil exist?" It is believed that God is pure and divine and that his light shines into the darkness with the ten rays of the Sefirot. When God's light does shine in the darkness, it is said that new worlds are formed. The closer you decide to get to God, the more his light will shine in your world and the less evil you'll have to deal with. The Qliphoth are the epitome of chaos and darkness, which held sway until God formed the light. These are the emanations of darkness in their personality forms:

- Thaumiel (ruled by Satan and Moloch)
- Ghagiel (ruled by Beelzebuth)
- Sathariel (ruled by Lucifuge)
- Gamichicoth (ruled by Astaroth)
- Golachab (ruled by Asmodeus)
- Thagirion (ruled by Belfegor)
- Arab-Zaraq (ruled by Baal)
- Samael (ruled by Adramelech)
- Gamaliel (ruled by Lilith)
- Nahemoth (ruled by Naamah)

Chapter Four: The Power of the Name of God

Before getting into the power of the name of God, it's important to address the divinity of the Hebrew language. First, Hebrew is known as "the Holy Tongue," or Lashon Hakodesh. For one thing, no words in Hebrew can be used to describe semen, excreta, private parts, or sexual acts, as observed by Maimonides. The Hebrew language refers to these things through figures of speech. However, according to Nachmanides, it's the Holy tongue because this was the language chosen by God to reach out to his people through the prophets of old.

Hebrew is known as the Holy Tongue.

Hebrew is a powerful language. The Torah makes it clear that before the occurrence at the Tower of Babel, everyone on Earth had the same language, and that language was Hebrew. Thanks to this language, those building the Tower of Babel could make it as far as they did to begin with. So, to keep them from building the tower until it reached heaven, God decided to scramble their languages, which is how the many languages we know today came to be.

Hebrew as the Language of Creation

The Book of Genesis discusses how God created the entire world. He said, "Let there be light," and there was light. Most people who read this passage assume that it is only rhetoric. However, the truth is that the words spoken by God have energy that *formed the light.* In the Torah, you will find ten phrases like the one he uttered described. These phrases are known as the Ten Utterances and are responsible for the world's creation. There isn't a single thing in existence that was not created with the power in those Hebrew words.

Those who practice the Kabbalah say that the word of God is not like regular human speech. When you speak common words, they are gone forever and accomplish nothing. However, the spoken word of God is everlasting. In the Book of Psalms, you will find a verse that says, "Forever, O God, your word stands in the heavens." This implies that God's Ten utterances are still at work in the heavens. Those utterances continue to give the world energy and vitality, recreating it as needed. Everything in existence is created through the power of words. Therefore, the Hebrew name of all objects carries the energy that sustains the existence of each one.

The Paradox

If you've followed so far, you may have noted a paradox. On the one hand, Maimonides says that excreta, semen, sexual organs, and acts don't have Hebrew words to describe them because they are vulgar. On the other hand, everything in the world exists thanks to the energy of its Hebrew name, which powers it. Therefore, shouldn't these so-called nasty things have Hebrew names too? Therefore, wouldn't that imply that the vulgar and profane are holy, as postulated by Nachmanides?

To figure out this conundrum, it is important to dive into Maimonides' musings about reality before sin and after sin. Before the sin of Adam and Eve, where they ate of the Tree of Knowledge of Good and Evil, sex and sexual organs were no more special than any other organs or human activities, and there must have been names for them in the Holy Hebrew language. However, after the fall of Adam and Eve, when they'd both become aware of the sensuality they had, these organs became connected to the sin of lust automatically. Therefore, there's no way to know their actual names since the concept of them being holy is beyond human understanding. However, both Nachmanides and Maimonides agreed on the fact that sexuality could either be profound or profane. It all comes down to context and intent.

To summarize the point about the holiness of the Hebrew language, Rabbi Yeshayah ha-Levi Horowitz (Shaloh) has said that when it comes to the alphabet and words of other languages, they are the creations of man. However, the Holy Tongue is special in that the name, sound, and even the shape of each letter of the Hebrew alphabet have spiritual characteristics and unique energies. So holy is Hebrew that the Zohar claims that speaking in the Holy Tongue causes the Divine Presence or Shechinah to rest on you. However, since the language is so holy, it is often only spoken when used to study or teach the Torah and to pray.

While learning how to *speak* in Hebrew for prayer, learning and studying are more important; it matters deeply that you understand the words coming out of your mouth. You need to understand the meaning of the words you *read*. This is why the Talmud is in Aramaic, and if you don't understand Hebrew properly, it's best to do your prayers in the language you know best.

The Names of God

Ein Sof happens to be just one of many names for the Creator. God's true, complete name is Shem HaM'phorash in Hebrew. Sometimes, it is written as Shem HaMephorash, Shem ha-Mehporash, or Schemhamphoras. This name means "the explicit name," and it was originally a Tannaitic description of God's hidden name in the Kabbalah and other more mainstream Jewish ideologies. This name has either 4, 12, 22, 42, or 72 letters. Sometimes the letters are written in triads.

Now, on to the versions of God's name with 12, 22, and 42 letters. Maimonides believed that Shem HaM'phorash was only used for the 4-letter name of God or the Tetragrammaton, which is either spelled JHVH or YHWH, pronounced as Jehovah or Yahweh. You'll find the 12-letter form of God's name in the Talmud, but it wasn't known to the Kabbalah and wasn't found in Jewish mysticism. The variant of God's name with 22 letters was first written in Sefer Raziel HaMalakh as Anaktam Pastam Paspasim Dionsim. The name's origins in this form aren't known, and there's no clear connection to Aramaic or Hebrew, at least none that has been found yet. There's also no way to conclude that its roots are Zoroastrian or Greek. However, Generic connections suggest the name predates the Sefer Raziel itself.

Hai Gaon described a 42-letter form of God's name and said while the consonants of God's name are known to one and all, the actual pronunciation isn't. Some say the first part of the name is Abigtaz. Others as Abgitaz. Some call the last part Shekuzit, while others call it Shakvazit. The different variations in the name could indicate that this version is rather ancient, so the Hebrew vowels have been lost over time. It comes from the first 42 letters in the Hebrew Bible and can also be found in the Sefer Raziel HaMalakh.

God's 72-Fold Name

Finally, there's the 72-fold name of God, which is of grave significance to Sefer Raziel HaMalakh. This name comes from the Book of Exodus, Chapter 14, verses 19 to 21. It is read boustrophedonically (from right to left and left to right) to give 72 names. Each of these names has only three letters. Rashi and the Sefer HaBahir from circa 1150 to 1200 explain how the method of getting these names works. According to the Kabbalah, the 72-fold name helped Moses cross the Red Sea, and it's said that this name can give holy men the power needed to perform miracles (like healing the six), casting out demons, stopping natural disasters, and killing enemies. It is also said that this sacred name can be used to create golems. As you've probably already figured, the point is that there's power in Hebrew letters and power in the names of God.

These 72 names aren't to be thought of as common names like Drew or Dave or Daisy, but they are 72 sequences of three Hebrew letters each that have the power to defy all the laws of nature and human nature. This was a formula written in code in the portion of the Bible describing the parting of the Red Sea. It's a secret no priest, Rabbi, or other Jewish mysticism scholar knew about. Only a few Kabbalists were aware of it, and they waited for the right time to share it with one another. You don't need to know how to speak Hebrew to enjoy the power of these names in your life. Each name acts as an index to certain spiritual energies or frequencies. Just looking at the letters or bringing them up in your imagination can connect you to those frequencies so that you can repair your soul as needed. Sometimes, the attribute "el" or "yah" can be added to the names to give you the names of the Geniis (the 72 Angels).

The shapes, sequences, sounds, and vibrations of each name have a light that purifies your heart and soul, eliminating the destructive flaws in your nature. The energy of these names is sacred and banishes anxiety, fear, and other detrimental emotions. So powerful are the Hebrew letters that the very word for letter in Hebrew means vibration or pulse, showing there is indeed a flow of energy when these words are spoken. The Hebrew alphabet is above and beyond geography, race, religion, and language. The three letters in each name can be thought of as having a positive charge, a negative charge, and a necessary ground wire to allow energy to flow. If you take advantage of the power in God's name, you should know the spiritual symbolism of each letter and number. A fantastic book on how to use God's names is The 72 Names of God: Technology for the Soul.

The Names of God

Just because God's names are too holy to be spoken in vain doesn't mean they should be lost from a lack of use to the sands of time. So it's essential to know them and know what they mean. God's names help everyone understand the different aspects of God and can help you with your magical practices. You should also study the spiritual symbolism of each letter to help you make the most of your prayers and practice using God's name. With that said, here are some of the names of God you can use in prayer and magic – and their meanings.

Yahweh: The one who has always existed and will keep on existing. The self-existent one needs nothing and no one to permit him to exist. This means you can lean on him whenever you need strength or someone to back you up.

Adonai: The King of kings and Lord of lords who reigns supremely. Therefore, calling on this name will force all authorities, principalities, and powers, causing you trouble to bow to the one and only God and do as you ask.

Yahweh Maccaddeshem: The Lord who sanctifies. This is the God who is able and willing to forgive all sin and to grant his Holy Spirit to you so that you can become as pure and loving as he is in all your ways.

Yahweh Rohi: The Lord who is your shepherd. You have no reason to want or lack anything. God takes care of you as a shepherd cares for their sheep. He keeps you from getting lost, hungry, thirsty, or having any unmet needs. This is the God who takes you to still, calm lakes, and gives you the fat of the land so you can experience abundant life. Use this name when you have needs you need to meet.

Yahweh Shammah: The ever-present Lord. He chooses to remain with you and won't forsake you. He is your best friend and confidant forever, and you can trust him not to betray you. This is excellent when you're on your own and need someone on your side.

Yahweh Rapha: The Lord, your healer. If you're ever going through health issues, whether mental, physical, emotional, or spiritual, you can call on God with this name to come to your aid.

Yahweh Tsidkenu: The Lord your righteousness. This name is excellent because it reveals the truth: You may be flawed, but through God, you can find yourself forgiven, purified, and perfect in his image.

Yahweh Jireh: The Lord is your provider. If you ever find yourself lacking or having needs that desperately need to be met, this is an excellent way to call on God for guaranteed assistance.

Yahweh Nissi: The Lord, your banner. This means you're not alone, no matter what you try to accomplish. You have backup from the Divine Creator himself. You will get victory in whatever you set out to do using this name, whether it's spiritual warfare or another challenge you face in the physical world. The Bible speaks of the Lord raising a banner of his love over you and covering you when the enemy wants to overwhelm you, much like a flood. Use this name when you want God to fight on your behalf.

Yahweh Shalom: The Lord, the peaceful one. Whenever you're dealing with strife or issues that have you constantly biting your nails in anxiety, that's the perfect time to call on Jehovah Shalom. He will act as the calm in the eye of the storm, keeping you sane while everything and everyone else falls apart. He will give you "the peace that passes all understanding," acting as your shield, strength, and shelter.

Yahweh Sabbaoth: He is the God in charge of the hosts of angels beyond numbering. These angels are mighty, destroying hell's armies with ease, as well as those who would attempt to mess with God's anointed one (that's you). You can call on Jehovah Sabbaoth when you need divine firepower to help you get through enemies' attacks.

Yahweh Ghmolah: The Lord of recompense. God's word says, "Vengeance is mine. I will repay." When you've been wronged, willfully hurt by someone, or mistreated, you don't have to waste your energy or time going after them. Call on Jehovah Ghmolah to come to your defense, and watch as the other person pays for everything they've done to you. Stand still and watch God restore everything you lost.

Elohim: The almighty and powerful Creator. He is the Lord of all, he who is above all others. He has power and might be beyond anything you could ever imagine. When you're dealing with a situation or a person that has you feeling completely defeated, call on Elohim.

El Elyon: The Highest God. Is there something or someone in your life that you find intimidating? Don't despair. Call on El Elyon, and every knee must bow before him on your behalf. No one is higher or greater than him, and all must acknowledge his authority. Exercise his divine power by using this name.

El Gibhor: This is the God of Might who can save one and all. It doesn't matter what you're dealing with. There's power in this name to help you overcome it all.

El Olam: The Lord the everlasting. All else is temporary, but he lasts forever. Your struggles, obstacles, and problems are temporary. God outlasts them all, and so does his love for you. The promises he has made you are everlasting as well. When you feel yourself losing faith because of whatever you're facing at the moment, don't despair. Use this name to remind yourself that God wins every time and is not about to stop winning on your behalf.

El Roi: The Strong One who sees all. Sometimes, you may feel like no one knows what you're going through or that no one actually sees you. Know that he does. He is with you and knows you even better than you know yourself. He knows your heart's desire, and because of his infinite love for you, he will do all he can to bring you to a good place. Trust him.

El Shaddai Rohi: The Lord, the one true God. Use this name when someone in your life has set themselves up in a position of power to torment you. It will serve as a reminder that you answer to no one but the Creator, who will surely put that person in their place. You can also use this name to address situations that have taken up so much of your time, energy, and resources.

El Chuwl: The Lord who gave birth. God is your Father. He knew you and loved you before you were born. The Creator has plans for you, and even if at the moment you may not be able to see them clearly, or it may feel like you're on your own, you're not. Trust him, and he'll make your life beautiful.

El Deah: Call this name when you need wisdom, knowledge, and understanding. It means "God of Knowledge." Attempting to be wise on your own will never work. You must reach out to God and learn from him by keeping his commandments. You should also listen to the messages he has for you and trust what he says.

Attiyq Youm: God, the Ancient of Days. He is eternal and has existed before, which means he has all power and authority over everyone and everything. Invoke God's power with this name when you need to get results that aren't forthcoming because of difficult people or situations.

Chapter Five: Angels and Their Hierarchy

Angels in Judaism are known as the Mal'akim (single form, mal'ak). It means "messenger." These angels are supernatural beings, and you can find mention of them in the Tanakh (the Hebrew Bible), writings from different rabbis, pseudepigrapha (falsely attributed texts), and apocrypha. These angels have different hierarchies; according to the Talmud, their energy is fire.

According to the Tanakh, each Patriarch of the Jewish faith had angels appear to them. Hagar, Lot, Abraham, Joshua, Moses, and others had witnessed angels. They went up and down Jacob's ladder in the Book of Genesis and showed themselves to Jacob. An angel also got in Balaam's way in the Book of Numbers. Isaiah the prophet talked about the angel of presence, also called the mal'ak panav, in the Book of Isaiah; in this book, Isaiah spoke about how he saved God's people. The Book of Psalms also discusses how God assigns angels to care for his people.

The Origin of Angels

The angel of the Lord has been perceived by generation after generation, yet the image of this being is not easily deduced. In the Tanakh, the angel tends to show up in a certain way: First, there's a narrative introduction of this being. The Angel of the Lord is usually portrayed as a deity in certain books of the Bible, such as when he assured fertility in Genesis, Chapter 21, verse 18. Another instance of the being acting as a deity is in the Second Book of Kings, Chapter 19, verses 32 to 26, where he demonstrated his might by wiping out an army with a single blow. Then there are times when the being speaks as though he were the one true God, like in chapter 3 of Exodus, verses 2, to 4. Then those who interact with this angel tend to act reverently toward the being as if they were a deity. This causes one to wonder if it was just an angel or God himself who showed up at those times.

Roles of Angels

They help with healing. There are instances in the Bible where the angels could heal people from impurity, but some wonder if the Seraphim would qualify as angels. For instance, Isaiah the prophet saw them praising God, and according to his account, they had such powerful voices that they caused the pivots on thresholds to rattle, and the whole temple was full of smoke. This is according to the Book of Isaiah, Chapter 6, verses 3 to 4. Their power was so intense that the prophet couldn't help but feel he wasn't worthy or clean enough to be in their presence, let alone witness their splendor. Then one of the Seraphim came to him and touched his mouth with a burning coal from the altar. Thanks to the angel, the prophet Isaiah discovered that he didn't have to worry about the things he'd done and said in the past. He had been forgiven, and all had been forgotten as soon as the burning coal came in contact with his lips. In the Book of Zechariah, Joseph had to be present before God and the being known as the angel of the Lord (Joshua 3:3). Also, when Zechariah had to be in their divine presence, it was clear to one and all that his clothes were in dire need of washing. So on the angel's command, Zechariah stripped and then put on the clothes that had been presented to him. The new set of clothes was clean, fit for all celebrations to come, but more than just being clean, they were a metaphor. The angel let Zechariah know that the process of changing out of the old clothes into the new ones meant that he no longer had to deal with the guilt and shame of his past, and therefore, you could see this as a true, healing miracle. How many souls are plagued by the wrongs they've done in the past? Imagine being able to move past all of that and start anew. This was the gift offered to Zechariah, and as he took it, so should you as a practicing Jew. The New Testament also talks about an angel that would come and trouble the waters at a certain fountain so whoever got in could be healed of whatever afflictions they had.

They help with prayer: In the Book of Zechariah, God lets Zechariah know that he's upset with his ancestors because of their terrible actions. He promised that if they were to come back to him, he would come back to them too. God's angel then decided to take it upon himself to advocate for the people God was so upset with. He said a prayer for them. In that prayer, he asked God to be clear about how long he felt it was okay to remain upset with and to continue punishing the people of Jerusalem and Judah because their relationship had taken hit after hit for seven decades, and it only made sense that God should eventually have mercy on them and make it possible to patch things up. Angels can pray on your behalf, too.

They go to war: Angels are not to be trifled with, as they are experts in matters of war. They are as fierce as they can be loving and understanding, and they are swift to uproot all evil machinations so that good can prevail. The Bible mentions four different visions of the end of the world, also known as the apocalypse, specifically in the Book of Daniel, which notes all the visions Daniel had. It talks about the battle between the Persian prince and Archangel Gabriel, who had informed Daniel there was no need to be alarmed since Archangel Michael was leading the charge against Persia and all would be well soon. So, Gabriel and Michael waged war against Persia for the sake of good. In Daniel Chapter 12, verse 1, Gabriel also says that Michael is responsible for protecting the Israelites from harm.

They pass on messages. Many passages from the Tanakh speak of angels acting as messengers. The truth is there's no actual Hebrew word that matches the English word "angel." These beings sometimes seem like regular humans, and usually, they are men. Unlike seraphim, they don't have wings. So it is important to note when a human messenger is being discussed in the Bible verses – and when it is an angelic messenger.

Despite all that, angels acting as messengers are vital because they serve as a connection between humanity and God and keep the needed space between the Creator and his creation. The angels carry heavenly, divine knowledge with them, and they can only share that knowledge with humans if God permits it and only if it is necessary to pass on a message. When an angel shares what God knows with those on Earth, that angel serves as God himself, and the angel's personal identity doesn't matter or exist in the process. The angel acts as God's very mouthpiece.

You can find many instances of angels serving as messengers in books of the Old Testament. Among them is the tale of the three mysterious men in the story of Sodom and Gomorrah (Genesis, Chapter 18, verse 1 to Chapter 19, verse 23). An angel also informed Samson's mother about the sort of baby she was to give birth to in the Book of Judges, Chapter 13, verses 3 to 5. The angels often had their identities disguised in these stories and were only about their job: Passing on a message.

Angels act as teachers: In the apocalyptic writings, there are stories about angels being teachers, especially in the Books of Daniel, Zechariah, and Ezra. Here, some people had the privilege of seeing prophetic visions (some terrifying, others mysterious). These people needed guidance to understand what they had just witnessed. So, the angel explained the visions so the prophet could grasp what they had seen, and they, in turn, could share more accurate knowledge about the end times with his people.

The angel's knowledge about the apocalypse had implications that affected both heaven and Earth and was very important to the Israelites, who were oppressed at the time and needed to understand why God was doing nothing about their situation. The angels embody heaven's might and God's authority, while they possess the warmth and love necessary to comfort the humans and remain relatable.

Hierarchies of Angels in Judaism

Rabbi Moshe ben Maimon, also known as Maimonides, talks about how there are 10 different hierarchies of angels, which he wrote about in Mishneh Torah around 1180. Here are the angelic rankings from the highest to the lowest. Note that other mystical texts may have different hierarchies, numbering more or less than 10. However, Maimonides' version is the most important one.

1. **Chayot ha Kodesh:** These angels are enlightened and responsible for upholding God's throne and ensuring the Earth remains in its rightful place in space. These angels emit powerful light, making them look like flames of fire. One of the famous angels in this

ranking is the archangel Metatron. Metatron is in charge of the Chayot ha Kodesh, according to the Kabbalah, and it happens that he is the archangel of Keter.

2. **Ophanim:** The Ophanim never sleep. This is because they are responsible for keeping watch over God's throne. They are also an incredibly wise group of angels, and their name comes from the Hebrew word *ophan,* meaning "wheel." The Torah talks about them in the first chapter of Ezekiel, saying that their spirits are housed in wheels that they use to move wherever they want. Archangel Raziel is in charge of these angels and is connected to the Chokhmah Sefirah.

3. **Erelim:** The Erelim are among the bravest angels under the rulership of archangel Tzaphkiel. These beings also happen to be quite understanding. They are known as the valiant ones and tend to show up when a national tragedy is about to happen or when death is imminent.

4. **Hashmallim:** The Hashmallim are very graceful, kind, and loving. They are led by archangel Zadkiel, according to the Kabbalah. Zadkiel is the one who was mercifully kind in the Book of Genesis, Chapter 22 when Abraham was just about to sacrifice Isaac, his son. This angel is connected to the Chesed Sefirah.

5. **Seraphim:** The Seraphim are the ones who are all about justice. According to the Kabbalah, archangel Chamuel leads the Seraphim. The Torah talks about a vision of the prophet Isaiah, where he saw the Seraphim around God in heaven. The Seraphim are six-winged creatures with two wings over their faces, two wrapped around their feet, and two for flight. Chamuel is also *Camael,* who is in charge of the Gevurah Sefirah.

6. **The Malakhim:** these are angels that are merciful and beautiful. They are led by archangel Raphael, connected to the Sefirah named Hod.

7. **The Elohim:** The angels in this ranking are all about having victory over evil. According to the Kabbalah, they are led by archangel Haniel

8. **The Bene Elohim:** These angels have the sole task of glorifying God. According to the Kabbalah, archangel Michael is in charge of this ranking. More than any other angel, Michael is mentioned

in different religious texts, and he is known to be a fighter and a warrior who wants nothing more than to win glory for God. In the Torah, he is known as "the great prince" who fights for those who love God daily in the battle of good versus evil and the world's end. Michael is connected to the Tiferet.

9. **The Cherubim:** These angels help people when they sin. They want nothing more than to make sure you don't get separated from God because of your sin, and they want you to be as close to God as you can. Gabriel's the one responsible for leading the Cherubim, who played a prominent part in the events after the fall in the Garden of Eden when sin became a thing on earth – thanks to the first man and woman succumbing to the serpent. After the fall of Man, it wasn't enough for God to chase the first couple out of the earthly paradise of Eden. To ensure no one would ever get back in and have access to the Tree of Life, God commanded a Cherubim to be on guard in eastern Eden, and there was also a sword engulfed in flames that zipped back and forth at the entrance. This made any attempt to get back in impossible and a fool's errand. This account is in the Book of Genesis, Chapter 3, verse 24. Remember, Gabriel oversees the Yesod Sefirah.

10. **The Ishim:** There's no other rank of angel as close to humans as the Ishim. They are all about constructing and uplifting the kingdom of God on Earth. They are led by archangel Sandalphon, who is connected to Malkuth.

Other Hierarchies

There are other hierarchies of angels that exist, according to the Zohar, Maselet Atzilut, Berit Menunchah, and Reshit Chochmah.

The Zohar Angelic Hierarchy

There are ten rankings of angels according to the Zohar. These are:

1. Malakim
2. Erelim
3. Seraphim
4. Chayot
5. Ophanim

6. Hashmallim
7. Elim
8. Elohim
9. Bene Elohim
10. Ishim

The Maseket Atzilut Angelic Hierarchy

According to Maseket Atzilut, written by Jacob Nazir, there are also ten rankings of angels, but in a different order than the previously mentioned ones. They are:

1. Seraphim
2. Ophanim
3. Cherubim
4. Shinanim
5. Tarshishim
6. Ishim
7. Hashmallim
8. Malakim
9. Bene Elohim
10. Elohim

The Berit Menuchah Angelic Hierarchy

According to Abraham ben Isaac of Granada, there are ten rankings of angels. He wrote about them in Berit Menuchah. They are:

1. Erelim
2. Ishim
3. Bene Elohim
4. Malakhim
5. Hashmallim
6. Tarshishim
7. Shinnanim
8. Cherubim

9. Ophanim

10. Seraphim

The Reshit Chochmah Angelic Hierarchy

Eliyahi de Vidas wrote Reshit Chochmah, and he also has ten rankings for these beings. Here they are from the highest to the lowest:

1. Chayot Ha Kodesh

2. Ophanim

3. Seraphim

4. Cherubim

5. Erelim

6. Tarshishim

7. Hashmallim

8. Elim

9. Malakim

10. Ishim

Chapter Six: The Teachings of Raziel

The archangel Raziel is the one who is closest to God. Also known as "God's Secret" or The Angel of Mysteries, and being the patron of lawmakers, judges, and lawyers, this archangel holds all the Universe's secrets and understands the mechanics of existence. He is also known as Akrasiel, Ratziel, Galluzur, and Saraquel. The mighty Raziel is a Prince of the Face, and he has several special tasks to perform in the kingdom of heaven. He's never far from God, which means calling on this angel will give you an extra advantage because you can get information that he's picked up in serving God so closely. It's impossible for mere mortals to figure out God's ways because Ein Sof is a mystery that's unknowable, and yet, Raziel may well be the one being who is privy to God's many secrets and actual feelings. Not only that, Raziel makes a point of being helpful to humanity by sharing anything he knows will assist you in life. Specifically, he loves to teach the fact that when it comes to manifesting your desires, all things take root in the world of spirit first before they shoot out into the physical world. Raziel may well be considered the original law of attraction teacher, as he shows one and all that all the thoughts we have are created spiritually and have no choice but to come to fruition in our lives.

Adam and Eve got access to the sacred Sefer Yetzir thanks to the Prince of the Face. They needed the information because life outside the garden of Eden was no picnic, and things had gotten terribly difficult for them. So in his mercy, Raziel decided he would do what he could to help, and he offered the duo his book. However, the other angels were not having it, and they took back the book. Rather than return it to its rightful owner, they decided it was best to let the ocean's murky depths have it forever. After this critical point in the story, you'll learn of other versions of what happened. For instance, some say Enoch found the book, and that was why he lived so long. It's also speculated that he edited the book to include important information about Metatron, a powerful archangel. After this, Raphael became the new owner of the book, then Noah, and finally King Solomon.

Others say that God was sad on behalf of Adam and Eve, and he really wanted to help them. So he commanded Rahab to search the ocean for the book and give it back to the duo. Depending on who you ask, Rahab is seen as an angel or a demon of the deep blue seas. From there, the book was passed on to Enoch, who gave it out as though it were his own work (the Book of Enoch). The next person to own it was Noah, and then it wound up with Solomon, who used it to gain knowledge about magic and manifestation.

The Many Faces of Raziel

Many things can be said of Raziel, but he's well known as the one in charge of the second heaven. Thanks to him, knowledge becomes wisdom. He's shown as a wizard, old and wise, and considered the patron of wisdom. He holds all the knowledge and wisdom and is excellent at teaching those who seek him how to remain focused. He is also good at helping you align with your Higher Self so you can find the connection between you and the wisdom of the Divine. He also shows up as an old man with remarkably huge wings resembling an eagle and a halo that resembles a rainbow. Sometimes he's got a gray, flowing robe, blue wings, and a yellow aura or halo floating around his head. He's the one who understands God's edicts, and he comes to the world so we can learn how to return to the Creator.

The Archangel Raziel is responsible for helping everyone remember important knowledge collected over the ages, including knowledge from previous incarnations. He's the one to call on when you have painful memories that linger and want to move past terrible trauma. If you had made promises in your past lives to people, Raziel could help you break the soul ties so you can be free, and he can also help you become prosperous in life, seeing as he's one of the Angels of Prosperity.

Archangel Raziel in Ancient, Sacred Writings

According to the Kabbalah, Raziel is the patron of Divine Wisdom and the embodiment of it. In other words, he is the Chokmah, the second of the ten holy Sefirot. The Kabbalah holds that Raziel is one of the ten archangels of the Briatic world, the second world of the four created. Rabbinic lore holds that he's the one who penned the Book of Raziel the Angel, or Sefer Raziel HaMalach. In this book, he talks about heaven and earth's deep secrets and mysteries, explaining them in detail. Within the pages of this book is all the knowledge that has ever and will ever exist, in heaven, on earth, and all other realms between. Some speculation exists about the actual author of the book. There are those who claim the author wasn't a divine being, but Eleazer of Worms, while others argue it's Isaac the blind. Many other characters could be responsible for writing the book, including Abraham ben Samuel Abulafia, who had opted for the pseudonym "Raziel and Zechariah. Depending on who you ask, the accounts state that Raziel never gave the first man his book but offered him the Zohar. Those who believe this claim that Hadraniel was the one who God sent to Adam and Eve to let them know the importance of keeping the book and its contents a secret. They were instructed to be careful because it wasn't a good idea to let any of the angels know they had the book with them. Their son Seth became a prophet with great power because Adam let him have the book.

The Legends of the Jews talks about how Noah became so knowledgeable about building arks and how it was thanks to Sefer Raziel, the holy book full of secrets. The archangel Raziel also shows up in Targum Ecclesiastes, explaining the secrets of life to all who will listen each day on Mount Horeb. Look in the Mishneh Torah, and you'll see this angel is there as well, acting as the leader of the Erelim. Some know him as God's own herald, others as the one meant to keep safe the realms unknown and all Ein Sof's mysteries.

It is believed that Noah learned to build his ark from the holy book of secrets.
Currier and Ives, CC0, via Wikimedia Commons
https://commons.wikimedia.org/wiki/File:Noah%27s_Ark_MET_DT1929.jpg

The Sefer Raziel

His book is mentioned once in the Zohar. There, it says that the middle of the Sefer Raziel has a secret writing encoded and that the passage contains 1,500 keys to unlocking the world's mysteries. No one, not even the angels of heaven, knows these keys. This book appears in several other texts, and the fact that it was continually handed down is a clue that there were powerful secrets in it. Other interesting details you can find in the book are the hierarchies of the hosts of heaven and their various purposes, which are essential for all of life to work the way it should. There are also angels that are connected to each sign of the Zodiac. Ovavorial, Lehetial, and Pheniel are connected to Aries, Taurus, and Gemini, respectively. Zorial, Berequiel, and Cheial are the angels affiliated with Cancer, Leo, and Virgo, also respectively. Gabriel's in charge of Scorpio, Medonial rules Sagittarius, and Capricorn is handled by Shenial. Gabriel also rules Aquarius, while Pisces is the domain of Romial. There are at least 70 other angels named in the book. It talks about the lives of the angels, what they are supposed to do, and more. So it's a great source of information on angels. It is believed that Raziel also had another book, the Sefer HaRazim, which he handed to Noah and is known as "the Book of Secrets."

The Book of Raziel the Angel has five sections that deal with the interactions between the angelic author and Adam right after the Fall. Adam had apologized for betraying God, which was why God was moved enough to send Raziel to him. Raziel taught Adam many things, including the proper way to speak and how thoughts have power that has very real effects on both the physical world and your spirit. He teaches about nature's laws, the planets, the way of life on earth, and what life is like in the astral realm. One of the most important teachings the angel had for Adam was how, even though the human soul is enclosed within the physical flesh, it remains a critical path to finding the balance between spiritual and physical realms while living on this planet. Raziel also shared critical information about the Hebrew alphabet and how to work with the 22 letters in magic.

Taking inspiration from various texts, especially the Sefer Yetzirah and the Sefer HaRazim, the Sefer Raziel talks about how all creation and energy start from God-inspired thoughts, which make their way from spirit to physical and manifest through action and speech. The book also shares information about God's names, how to use the stars and the Zodiac in magic, perform protective spells, and work with amulets to heal oneself and others.

Practical Magic

There are various teachings you can learn in Kabbalah as a whole, and when it comes to Kabbalah Ma'asit (Practical Kabbalah), there's much more to absorb. This aspect of Kabbalah is about using magic in practical ways — specifically white magic, not black magic, which is verboten. The tradition of Kabbalah Ma'asit involves chanting the divine names of holy angels, working with amulets, performing divinations, and soothsaying. One of the sacred texts relevant to this tradition is the Sefer Raziel HaMalakh, or the Book of Raziel the Angel.

So, what is this book, really? A single text that's rather long, speaking about all the knowledge there is to be had, from astrology to the secrets of creation on earth. It talks about birth, death, reincarnation, and the life cycle, among other deeply spiritual matters. This book alone is responsible for the difference between mainstream Kabbalah (Kabbalah

Iyunit) and Practical Kabbalah. The former is about trying to understand what God is like and what existence is about. It's about working with a belief system that involves several discourses on God and meditative methods. However, the Practical Kabbalah is about something more. It's about the process of creating using magic and how to reach out or summon the angels and God himself. However, the sacred texts usually condemn working with magic, saying it's evil, so there needed to be a fine distinction between the devil's evil magic and the pure magic of Practical Kabbalah. The practical and theoretical differences are why Practical Kabbalah hasn't been practiced by many other than the Jewish elite.

Using Raziel's Teachings: Working with Thought and Imagination

If there's one powerful thing to take away from the Sefer Raziel, it's that thoughts have power. This is no longer a secret, but despite how often people hear this, they clearly don't put it into practice. Think about how automatic your thoughts are in reaction to things. When something bad happens, notice how quickly you expect more bad things to happen or worse outcomes than what is present. It's very easy to look at things as they seem and assume that's all they will ever be. It's easy to assume that if there's to be any change, it will only be for the worse. However, you've got to master your thoughts. The first step is finding the space between what triggers those less-than-desirable thoughts and your response. You need to stop reacting and start being deliberate about your response, and to do that, you should practice meditation regularly. The more you meditate, the less reactive you will be to occurrences, and the more you'll realize you can choose how you respond — or not to respond at all.

The next thing that one needs to do, in keeping with Raziel's revelation about how thoughts create things, is to practice *thought substitution*. In other words, the next time your mind is tempted to go somewhere, that will only lead to the creation of undesired circumstances, pause and deliberately replace that thought with something you'd prefer to happen. You can either do this each time an errant thought pops up or set time aside each day to see your life or the situation you're dealing with go exactly as you'd prefer. Then, when you see or experience things that point to the contrary throughout your day, return to the memory of your visualization, and learn to accept it as done. By practicing this with all things big and small each day, you'll start to notice the archangel really was correct about the fact that *thoughts create things*. For best results, you should ensure you calm down and relax your body and mind before substituting bad thoughts with preferred ones.

Also, make sure to visualize things that could only happen after you've accomplished what you want, not what happens in the process. For instance, if you want a new car, see yourself driving the car after having it for three months rather than seeing yourself go into the dealership to pick out the car.

Finally, ensure you're playing a part in your mind, just like acting in a movie. Don't imagine yourself from a third person's perspective, or the odds are someone else will get what you envisioned in real life while you're left with nothing. Don't see yourself behind the steering wheel of the car. Instead, see the road ahead, your hands on the wheel, the dashboard in front of you, and so on. **Be in the first person when you think these thoughts.**

Using Raziel's Teachings: Pathworking Ritual for Prosperity and Peace

The ritual is a simple one. Before you start, you must know what you want from the ritual, or it will do nothing for you. Start by writing a request, keeping it a simple statement in the present tense. Assume, for instance, you have been struggling with bad luck in business, and you want to be protected from it. You could write, "Sitael, keep me safe from all that would cause me harm." Don't define how the angel you want to summon should do its job, or the ritual will probably fail because of the constraint you've put on the angel. You must ensure you phrase your intention in the present tense, *not the future* because using the future tense means your goal will always be sometime in the future. You know the saying: Tomorrow never comes. Note that the attitude you have towards this ritual is important. If you assume what you're doing is silly, that means you won't get results.

Here's how the ritual goes:

1. Imagine being in a dark cave.

2. Imagine a waterfall is at the cave's mouth in the distance, and you're now close enough to see the light from the cave's exit.

3. Imagine the sun shining through that magnificent waterfall, forming rainbows. You're still in the dark at this point.

4. Next, imagine you're in a forest full of pine trees and bedazzling light. Feel the light bathing your body, then say, "Raziel." You may notice something immediately or gradually, seeing Raziel or sensing his presence. Either way, don't force it.

5. If nothing happens, you may repeat Raziel's name, not as a mindless mantra but as though you were calling a friend over from the next room. You may do this with your mental voice, which should be clear and loud enough for anyone on the other side of the forest to hear you. You could do this aloud if you prefer. Spend no more than five minutes doing this, and if you haven't received an actual answer, just accept that Raziel is now with you. If you notice her strong presence, stay calm, and don't give a speech about not being worthy.

6. Ask Raziel to lead you to Sitael (or any other angel you'd like to work with). Speak as if you're talking with an old friend you're comfortable with and would be happy to show you where your mutual friend (Sitael, in this case) is.

7. After this, it's time to perform the pathworking for Sitael. Imagine a sword on the ground. It doesn't matter what it looks like. Just see it there.

8. Next, imagine a serpent sliding over the sword.

9. Next, see a field of green grass in your mind's eye, and notice the blue sky.

10. Next, see a tower reach into the sky. This tower is strong and clearly sturdy. It doesn't matter what it looks like, but it has to be obviously built to last, and it must reach into the sky.

11. Call Sitael. Say the name confidently, even if you're not sure you're pronouncing it right. What matters here is your intention. Don't be concerned about doing things wrong regarding rituals like this.

12. If you don't see or feel Sitael's presence, you can call his name several times, either in song or by repeating it. Do this for just five minutes.

13. Whether you had an actual reply or response or not, it's time to make your request. First, think about what you want from the angel. Ensure you feel how much you want it. You want to feel it strong enough that the angel has an idea of how much you want it, but don't feel constrained to drum up deep emotions if you can't manage that.

14. Next, state what you want from Sitael. You may get a response as a flash of an image or feel like the angel needs more information. You just need to trust what you get. You can speak with the angel like a friend. If you want information, it helps to pause after asking to see what you get.

15. After making your request, it's time to end the ritual. Thank Sitael (or whichever angel you just worked with) and Raziel. Then, imagine yourself being back in the dark cave. Don't skip this step.

16. As soon as you're back in the cave, stop imagining and do your best to completely forget and let go of the ritual you just did. Trust that the answer you want will come when you need it, and let it go.

Chapter Seven: Kame'ot or Magical Jewish Amulets

The amulet is one of the most vital magic tools in Jewish mysticism and Practical Kabbalah. The Hebrew word for amulet is *kame'a* (plural: kame'ot). In the Sephardic world, many landmark events were marked with folk practices. More often than not, the Jewish scholars and leaders seek to put down folk practices so that they are not tied to superstitious beliefs, but when you pay close attention, you'll notice that the practices in question were part of the fabric of the Sephardic way of life, shed light on the values and concerns of the collective and the individual, and provided useful methods to deal with stressors and anxiety. The Hebrew word *kame'a* suggests that the practice of making and wearing amulets is connected to the concept of binding or tying.

For instance, certain practices became more common during pregnancy. If you were part of the Sepharadim, while you love nothing more than when a new child is born, odds are you're also scared about the danyadores – evil spirits or demons that could threaten the wellbeing of the baby to come. Jewish communities worldwide, whether Sepharadim or Ashkenazim, know that there are things to do to keep the effect of the evil eye away from one's baby and life. A common practice when dealing with pregnant women or childbirth is to spit on a baby (or near them) and then say "poo poo" out loud as an exclamation meant to drive away the evil spirits. The mothers of Salonica had no option but to use special potions and incantations (mastered by the older women among them) to make sure they'd not only carry their babies to term but would deliver them with nothing going awry in the process. There's also a common Turkish practice where, as a pregnant woman, someone would put a sprig of rue by your head to keep you shielded from evil forces and the evil eye.

The Protective Kame'ot

Have you ever wondered how you can ensure you stay safe from such entities as demons? If you thought it was impossible, the fact is, *you can do this*. All you need are the kame'ot. These special, powerful amulets ward off all evil beings from you that may want to wreak havoc in your life. Historically, Jewish women were great at kantikas, but if you wanted a kame'ot, you'd have to go to the men. Some kame'ots would have special parchment put into them, and these are known as *shadayim*. They have the names of the angels written on them, as well as Lilith, who is a demon particularly fond of causing harm to newborns. If you were the mother of the child, you had no choice but to attach a shadayim to yourself and one to your child so that you could both be safe. Since Lilith is a winged being, the Kame'ot accounts for this by incorporating wings, too.

Old World Kame'ot

Back in the Ottoman times, it was common for scribes to craft kame'ot, but just because it was common doesn't mean the practice wasn't powerful. They had various ones that could help summon specific angels meant to protect babies. They would write down these spiritual formulas on special parchment, which is then folded to create a shape reminiscent of the Sephardic filla. Then the kame'a would have to be wherever the newborn is, even when they become adults. Depending on preference, the kame'a could be designed completely sealed off, with a string connected to it to allow you wear it as a pendant. Other times, it's just carried around in a bag or wallet. Some people truly believe that their kame'a is why they can handle all the trouble that comes their way.

New World Kame'ot

Avraham Maimon left his beloved hometown of Tekirag in 1924 because he wanted to be a Rabbi. He decided Seattle was a good place to make his home. He was responsible for keeping most of the Sephardic Studies Digital Collection of kame'ot, and he kept them in different scripts. What isn't clear is if he's the one who created them. If he did, it would imply he chose to forget about the evil spirits of old when he moved to the United States. Other Sepharadim who had moved to the States still continued to entertain the thought that demons could follow them to their new abodes, so they took their kame'ot seriously.

When it comes to Jewish amulets, they are different from others because there aren't that many symbols on them. The power behind them is the written word. The power also flows from God's names and the angels. For the most part, that's all the amulets draw on for power, but that doesn't mean you can't find other items in Judaism that can act as a magic cure or protection. Sometimes the amulets are fashioned out of stones or parchment. Other times, depending on what you prefer, they could be silver or metal, which means they last longer. Some of them are even cut from gems. There's no hard and fast rule about whether you need to wear it all the time or if you can just hang it up in your home.

Few of the amulets of old are still in production today. When they are, it's only by rare people in specific areas. Other than the Hand of God, most of these amulets are no longer part of popular Jewish practices. Sometimes amulets are really popular, and other times, they aren't. This has been the case over the centuries, depending on where and when. Sometimes, people thought they were nonsense, and other times they believed in them, but they weren't used the way they should be, according to most rabbis.

Approval for Amulets and Amulet Writers

Amulets were a deep cause for concern among religious authorities who didn't like them. Even if not everyone supported them, they have God's names and Torah passages, among other things, making them sort of sacred. They were too sacred to be casually worn or used (like on the Sabbath), yet not so sacred that one couldn't just let them burn in case of a fire outbreak. One thing was clear to the authorities: Amulets were here to stay, and the people weren't about to give them up for anything. So rather than fight the reality of the situation, the authorities simply chose regulation. This meant that before you could write or create amulets, you had to have their approval and verification. How? First, your amulet must have been used for at least three different circumstances by three different people, and it has to be proven as effective. Also, you couldn't just craft your amulet out of whatever materials you wanted. Working with clay, parchment, and metal was considered standard practice. All that mattered was that the parchment was kosher. The content of the amulet also needed to be approved. It wasn't okay to use the Torah's words to heal, but these days, it seems there's more leniency in that regard. It was also fine to protect with the words. As such, most amulets in circulation are more about prevention: Keeping one safe from miscarriage, bad luck, demons, the evil eye, and so on. Some amulets can be used to promote fertility, health, blessings, and favor.

Getting Ready for Amulet Writing

Actual amulet writers who know their craft and have been approved don't just write amulets. Say you write amulets yourself. You've got to get ready because you can't just jump straight into crafting them. There are prayers and rituals you must observe, and if your amulet happens to be made with parchment, you'd be held to stricter standards of preparation. You have to purify yourself, say special prayers, and be on a fast as you script the amulet. You also have to make sure you write any of God's names exactly as it appears in the Torah, and that each letter stands alone without touching the next one. All writing is to be done on the hairless side of the parchment, and before you even get to the writing process, you have to prepare and consecrate the ink for this purpose, too. The scribe also has to recite a blessing to God before writing. The amulet writers are known as *ba'ale shem,* which means "masters of the Holy Name."

Ayin Hara

Ayin Hara means "evil eye," and it's believed to be the source of pain, tragedy, sickness, and all the bad things that could befall one in the world. Often, the harm from the ayin hara results from jealousy, which is why there's a commandment that states one should never covet something that belongs to someone else. A common saying among the Jews is bli ayin hara, which means "without an evil eye." They also say ken eina hara, or keynahora which is Yiddish for "no evil eye," when they are discussing a good thing that just happened. For instance, if you were suddenly blessed with a new and better job than the one you had, you could share that news with your friend and end it by saying, "bli ayin hara."

According to Rashi's commentary, the Torah doesn't talk about the ayin hara, but there are several times the evil eye is at work. This was in the Book of Genesis, Chapter 16, verse 5. Here, Sarah gave Hagar the ayin hara because she was jealous of her ability to carry a child for Abraham, and this was why the maid miscarried. (Notably, she later became pregnant with Ishmael, but scholarly rabbis discovered that Ishmael was not her *first* pregnancy.) Later in Genesis, Chapter 42, verse 5, Jacob warns his sons that they shouldn't be seen together because that could cause a case of the ayin hara against them.

The Talmud and Kabbalah talk about the evil eye. In Pirkei Avot, Rabbi Yochanan ben Zakkai had five disciples offer advice on what they thought it meant to live a good life and stay away from evil. Each Rabbi had a different answer:

- A good eye
- A good friend
- A good neighbor
- To see the outcome of your actions
- A good heart

In response, the Rabbi told them that he preferred the answer given by Rabbi Eliezer, the son of Aroch. What was the answer he preferred? A good eye. He then told them to go and see the worst personality trait that one should stay as far away from as possible. He refers to the evil eye, which leads the heart to evil inclinations and causes one to hate others. There are several ways to stay away from the ayin hara or keep its effects far from you, but most of these are from non-Jewish traditions, dating back to the times of the Talmud when the Jews would have charms to ward off the ayin hara. Some of the ways Jews do this now include:

- Wearing a red thread on the wrist
- Wearing a hamsa or hanging it up at home
- Wearing a chai around the neck

The Red String

The red thread is a sign of vitality and life. The Hebrew word for red is adom, and the word for blood is dam, which is from the same root as the words for "watch," "adam," and "man," making up adamah. The red thread shows the strong connection between life and blood. There's a difference between the color red and the color known as shani. During the time of the Torah, a crimson dye came from a mountain worm known to infest the eastern Mediterranean trees. This insect is called the Torah's crimson worm or tola'at shani. The crimson worm has many connections to the color red and instances where people repented in the Torah, showing that something as insignificant as a slithering worm has an elevated status thanks to the process of repentance. Red is meant to ward off evil, so tying a red string on your wrist will naturally ward off the ayin hara.

The Hamsa Hand

This one sprung from the Middle East, and it looks just like your hand, but with only the three middle fingers pointed out while the other fingers curve outwards. The talisman can be worn as an amulet and offers protection from ayin hara. You may also hang this in your home. Hamsa means "five." It's about the fact that the hand has five fingers, and it's also a representation of the five books of the Torah. Some people call it Miriam's Hand, the hand of Moses' sister. Muslims call it *Fatima's Hand* in honor of Fatima, a daughter of Mohammed the Prophet. It also represents the Five Pillars of Isalm. Scholars think this hand is older than Islam and Judaism, possibly rooted in non-religious origins, but there's no certainty about that. All you need to remember is that kamiyot or Kame'ot represent the concept of binding, the Talmud doesn't outlaw them, and it's okay to have one on you when you're at the synagogue for Shabbat. Sometimes, the thumb and pinky are curved outwards. Other times, they are much shorter than the middle fingers, while they are always symmetrical. Also, there's usually an eye in the middle of the palm that acts as a potent talisman for keeping ayin hara at bay. Other symbols on Hamsa include Hebrew words and the fish, which is also a sign of good luck. Some Hands of Hamsa have mazal or mazel etched into them, and this is meant to represent the concept of good luck.

The Chai

Chai means living, and among the letters in its spelling are Chet and Yud. Some people pair the Chai with the Hamsa Hand, and others wear it with the Star of David. The word Chai is pronounced kai, with the k being guttural. It represents the value of being alive and the hope of seeing another day. It's about having the will to live and the drive to keep all life safe. This amulet can bring you good luck, prosperity, and more.

How to Make an Amulet

1. Get the Hamsa or chai. You can find these for sale online.
2. Cleanse the object by breathing on it thrice.
3. Bless the object with the energy you want to imbue it with.
4. Write the specific blessing or energy you want to carry with you on a piece of paper. You can use any Hebrew letters at this book's end.
5. Wrap the paper around your preferred amulet, then let it stay wrapped for three days and three nights.
6. Wear the amulet.
7. When you sense the energy is waning, you can wrap the amulet in the paper you used to charge it again, leaving it overnight. You can also just do that every night.

Chapter Eight: Rites, Rituals, and Shabbat

In Judaism, those who follow the path have to render service to God through having faith, studying his word, praying, being kind to one another, and following the Torah's commandments. Jewish rituals and holidays are all rooted in Halakha, which means "the path one walks." Halakha is Jewish Law. It's a foundation of commandments, rabbinic laws, and traditions. It's not just about religious life but everyday life, including what you wear, how you comport yourself, how you help the less privileged, and so on. The observance of these rites, rituals, and Shabbat is a way to demonstrate your gratitude to and love for God, making each day sacred and beautiful.

Jewish Cycle of Life Rituals

In Judaism, there are life cycle events that are held in high esteem, being honored year after year. Here are some of those events:

Brit milah is also known as *bris*. This is a word etymologically rooted in the Ashkenazic Jews dialect. The Ashkenazi are those who are European but not descendants of Iberia. Bris is the ritual that involves the circumcision of Jewish boys. Circumcision is the process of removing the penis' foreskin days after the birth of a Jewish boy – a practice coming from the story of Abraham's instructions from God to circumcise himself and then Isaac, his son. Once a male child is eight days old, he has to undergo this process (unless there's a medical reason he shouldn't). The bris is carried out by a practitioner known as a mohel. The child must be held by someone (usually the grandfather) who acts as the sandek. Being the sandek is considered a thing of prideAfter this ritual, the family has a meal to celebrate. The meal is called s'udah.

Simchat bat (Hebrew for "joy of a daughter") is a Jewish naming ceremony that is held for a baby girl on the day of her birth or on the first Sabbath after her birth. The ceremony is similar to a Brit Milah (circumcision) ceremony for boys.

During the Simchat Bat ceremony, the baby girl is given her Hebrew name and is welcomed into the Jewish community. The ceremony usually takes place in the synagogue, and family and friends are invited to participate. A Torah scroll is often present, and the baby girl is often held over the scroll as a way of symbolically bringing her under the protection of the Torah.

The ceremony includes prayers, blessings, and the recitation of traditional Hebrew prayers and psalms. The father, or another male relative, may give a short speech, and the baby's mother may also speak. Often, the baby is also blessed by the rabbi, and the parents and grandparents may give gifts to the baby.

Pidyon ha-ben is an interesting event indeed. According to tradition, the firstborn son must help in the Temple in Jerusalem. Since there's no present Temple, the requirement is more symbolic, but the traditional practice is to redeem the firstborn sons from the obligation they have to the Temple where and when possible. The children from families of priests (those born of Aaron, Moses' brother, also called the kohanim, singular kohen) and the Levite families have no choice but to perform their service. Other than that, the father of the firstborn son has to pay five silver coins to a kohen to set his child free once he is a month old. After the ritual, blessings will be recited, and there'll be a special meal.

Bar or bat mitzvahs are for masculine and feminine children, respectively. This is a ceremony that's already covered. It's about the fact that a Jewish child is now an adult. It happens when the boy turns 13 or when the girl turns 12. The ceremony occurs the same day as the birthday, usually during a synagogue service. The celebrant will have to wear a tallit or prayer shawl for the first time in their lives, and they'll have to come up for an aliyah for the first time. They also read from the

Pentateuch, and haftarah, part of a book of the prophets connected to the week's Torah portion. They also are meant to give a Dvar Torah, where they talk about what the week's Torah portion means to them. After all this, there's a party or a meal to celebrate.

Confirmation is a ritual that was developed not too long ago, in the 19th century. It's not an obligatory event and is more common with secular Jews. It represents that you've gone on with formal Jewish education, moving past the basic bar or bat mitzvah leve. There are several rituals done to mark this occasion, but usually, the confirmation class is witnessed in the synagogue. Religious gifts can be exchanged, and there's food to enjoy.

Marriage is a complex, intricate ritual when it comes to Judaism. Since there are several ways one could practice Judaism, and since each community treats cultural and religious events differently, you may find all sorts of variations in the practice of marriage. There are many ways that Jews look at non-heterosexual marriages, and these views they hold are still evolving. Trying to get into these views in this book will be too much, so the focus here will be on heterosexual marriages.

In Ashkenazic communities and many others, before the wedding, there's an aufruf. On the Shabbat before the wedding day, the groom is called to the Torah to receive blessings and honor. If the congregation is egalitarian regarding gender, the bride and groom will be called to the Torah. After this, the congregation will sing songs and throw candy at them to signify that they'll have a sweet married life together.

Just before the actual wedding, a ketubah is signed by two witnesses.

The wedding happens beneath a special canopy called a chuppah. This canopy has four poles, and the poles are a representation of the couple's marital home. As the bride, you have no choice but to cover your face with a veil. This is meant to be a reenactment of how Jacob wound up getting married to Leah rather than the one he really wanted: Rachel. To deceive Jacob, there was a veil on Leah's face, and by the time he found out she wasn't Rachel, it was too late. So as a bride, you've got to have a veil, and as a groom, you've got to take the veil off your bride's face to be sure you're getting married to the right partner. The bride has to walk around the groom three or seven times, depending on the community observing the wedding. After this, the groom offers the bride a ring or some other valuable things, and when it's an egalitarian wedding, both partners exchange these valuable gifts. To make the marriage formal, they need the sheva b'rachat, seven blessings. The groom must break a glass, too. If the wedding is egalitarian, both the bride and groom will break the glass, as a reminder that even amid joy, there can be sorry. This practice is a callback to the desecration and ruin of the Temple.

After the wedding, there'll be a party and a festive meal. It's also common for there to be dancing, particularly the hora. Also, there's a traditional practice of lifting the groom and bride in the air on chairs. After the meals, a special grace known as the birkat ha-mazon is recited.

Divorce is yet another event to consider in Judaism. It's not encouraged, but it's allowed. There needs to be a get, which is a document that legitimizes the divorce. According to Jewish law, the husband must offer his wife a get, freely, with no coercion. Tradition also holds that the bride has to choose to accept the get from him, although this is strictly a matter of tradition and not law. This can be an issue in Jewish communities that observe this practice, and as a result, there have been many possible solutions that are sometimes acceptable and other times not, depending on the community in question. These solutions can include prenuptial agreements, but there are fewer legal forms that offer more leeway and creativity every now and then.

Death is an event that cannot be avoided. In Judaism, when someone passes on, they are not embalmed. Instead, the body is washed in a ritual by the chevra kadisha or the "holy society," a bunch of people who will then go on to dress the body in tachrich (a linen garment). Then, the chevra kadisha will put the body into a simple wooden casket. There's to be no metal because the body must return to dust as soon as possible. The group also remains with the body as they recite from the Book of Psalms. When it comes to the funeral, there's no viewing option. It's okay to give eulogies, and you may recite from the Book of Psalms (Chapter 23, in particular.)

Mourning happens immediately after one hears of death. Traditionally, this is when someone recites the following blessing in Hebrew: Blessed are you, Lord our God, king of the Universe, the judge of truth. And then, after this recital, the mourner may rip their clothes. This tradition is sometimes replaced by the mourners wearing a ribbon during the funeral, which they tear symbolically. When the burial is over, it's time for shiva. This period lasts seven days when all are expected to mourn. In English, this is called "sitting shiva." At this time, the family of the one who passed on will receive visitors at their home, share memories of the deceased, pray with the community, and eat traditional comfort foods such as eggs. The mourners aren't about vanity at this time, and any grooming is minimal, at best. Mirrors are to be covered, and no one gets to wear anything fancy — *particularly leather.* They are also not allowed to attend or be part of anything joyous.

After the burial, there's the shloshim, which means "thirty," and lasts for 30 days once the burial is done. The mourners are meant to stay away from anything joyous.

Conversion is what happens when someone non-Jewish would like to convert to Judaism. To do this, you'll need a *beit din* to approve. The beit din is a Jewish rabbinical court. Note that Judaism isn't a movement that goes around trying to add to its numbers. Traditionally, the rabbi is meant to refuse a would-be convert thrice, and they are not to take them under their wing unless the student persists. As a convert, you're known as a ger (for the female, she is called a *giyoret*), and you must study Judaism before your conversion. You must also explain what's driving you to convert to the belt din, who must find your explanation satisfactory. After that, you'll need to immerse yourself in a ritual bath known as a mikveh.

There are various Jewish communities with different outlooks on conversion; some of them don't honor conversions done by rabbis outside their movement. Conversion is something you can do as a gentile if you want to get married to someone Jewish. You can also do this if you were raised Jewish but aren't technically a Jew (maybe because you have a Jewish dad but a non-Jewish mom).

Mikvah or mikveh is a ritual bath, and most Jewish communities have at least one. The law says that you must immerse yourself in this bath to convert to Judaism. Also, if you're a woman getting married, you must go in this bath first. There's also the practice of menstrual purity or niddah, which requires going in the bath. There are many reasons to do a mikvah, and the mikvah is open to men, women, and gender-nonconforming Jews. There's more to the mikvah than already mentioned, as this bath has great symbolism in Jewish tradition. Some Hasidic men practice getting into the mikveh daily, while others do so on

Fridays before Shabbat. Some Jewish communities require immersion in the mikvah before Yom Kippur, and others require grooms to go in the bath before getting married.

The mikveh immersions don't need blessings, and they may happen in a mikveh meant for men only, often large enough to contain ten or more men simultaneously. Since they are not necessarily required, most mikva'ot for men tend to be casual, and it could be run without having to schedule a bath as most men are walk-ins. Recently, some progressive Jews have marked special milestones in life with a mikveh, taking baths when there's a special birthday, graduation, bat, or bar mitzvah, and as a sign of starting fresh after loss or pain. For instance, you could take this bath after a year of mourning or dealing with abuse, divorce, rape, or some dangerous sickness you've recovered from. There are usually prayers that follow these baths. There's also the kelim mikveh, specifically meant for immersing dishes so they become kosher. This mikvah is smaller than the other kind and is usually housed in the same building as the larger mikvah.

Holy Days Throughout the Year

The Jewish calendar is lunisolar (keeping in sync with the natural cycles of the sun and moon), and it's used mostly for the Jewish holy days and other traditional observances. The calendar is used to figure out when holy days are meant to be observed. It's also used to indicate the dates for ceremonies like Torah readings, yahrzeits (to honor those who have passed on), Psalm readings, etc. The observances usually commence at sundown, before the date.

Rosh Hashanah is known as the "head of the year." The precise dates depend on when the first day of the seventh month of the Hebrew calendar falls. A special celebration is held during fall, specifically on Tishrei's first and second days. These dates could be anytime in September or October. Note that the Jewish and Western New Years are different on account of the fact that different calendars are used. It's a time for you to think about how your previous year was for you, see how you could have done better, and make a commitment to making the new year better than the previous one. You have ten days to do this, and after that is Yom Kippur. Work is forbidden during this time, and you celebrate the festival with some challah bread and honey, and apples. These sweet treats aren't just randomly chosen, but they are meant to be a sign to you to trust that the coming year will be a sweet one.

Yom Kippur rolls around on day ten of the month of Tishrei. Some call it the Day of Atonement, and just as it sounds, it happens to be the holiest day of the year, and fasting is to be honored with fasting, which is abstinence from food. If you intend to walk the Jewish path, you must realize that nothing matters other than to connect fully with Ein Sof, to find yourself whole in him by being merciful and compassionate to those who have done you wrong while you seek to be forgiven for your misdeeds, too. It's not enough to forgive and be forgiven, though, because you have to confess all sins to God, whose forgiveness is required as well. What's all this forgiveness about? It's about restoring broken relationships between one another and between yourself and God, who loves you. It also matters because, on this day, God comes to a conclusion about what your fate will be. It's a celebration that isn't as upbeat as the others, but it's still a happy and pleasant day because you're seeking to let go of old wrongs and wounds, so everyone can begin on a fresh page with one another.

Sukkot is a celebration that lasts for a full week, and some know it as the Feast of Tabernacles. It's a pilgrimage feast, a period during which the Jews offer their heartfelt thanks to God. Sukkot starts on the 15th of Tishrei. Also called the Feast of Booths, the ceremony is named after the huts or booths known as a sukkah, built solely for that purpose. They represent how the Israelites lived after escaping Egypt with Moses' help, wandering around for 40 years until they came to the promised land. The celebration kicked off as a harvest festival — an ancient one with many traditional practices meant to express gratitude for the bounty of the fall harvest. The sukkahs are made of thatched roofs or branches for the roof. These roofs offer shade from the sun during the day and a gorgeous night sky view. During this time, decorations go on the sukkah. Everyone has myrtle, citron, palm, and willow branches, and they shake them in honor of how God graciously blessed the Jews with the Holy Land and its gifts. If you're part of a Jewish home, it's customary to ask your forbears to share food with you and to stay in the sukkah for as long as possible for the week.

Shmini Atzeret and **Simchat Torah** are ceremonies that last two days. The holy days begin on the eighth day of Sukkot, making up a single holiday for most Jewish practitioners. In Israel, they are celebrated on the same day. The same goes for some Reform congregations, too. The night before both celebrations, the girls and women have to light candles while families say sacred blessings, go to services, and participate in the feasts that happen both night and day. It's unacceptable to do most kinds of work during this time. The event of Shmini Atzeret is when you enjoy your sukkah feast, and some challah is eaten with salt. Before the end of the next day, you enjoy another meal with your family and bid them goodbye after. Hakafot is an important tradition of the Simchat Torah where you and everyone else will march around the reading table in the synagogue while singing songs, both at night before the main event and the morning of the event. Typically, hakafot happens on the eve of Shmini Atzeret.

Chanukah is an eight-day event. Also known as the Festival of Lights, it begins on the 25th day of the month of Kislev, which will often fall in December. The word Hanukkah represents the concept of dedication, specifically celebrating the fact that Judah the Maccabee won a victory over one of Israel's most formidable oppressors, the Seleucids. It's also about the fact that the Temple had been rededicated after this, and it celebrates the story of how the oil lasted seven days longer than it should have in the temple. Chanukah is all about lighting the nine-flamed menorah each night. The entire synagogue and the families who showed up for Hanukkah have to place the menorah in a doorway or window and then pray to God. The middle flame is used to light up the others, with one flame being lit per night until the final night, as all flames burn. After this, the Jews sing songs and enjoy fried meals like sufganiyot and latkes to honor the miracle at the Temple.

Tu B'Shevat is held on the 15th day of Shevat, and it's also known as Rosh Hashanah La'llanot, which means "New Year of the Trees." It usually holds January or February, and it's the end of the rains and the start of the trees' new life cycle in Israel. According to law, this festival is for figuring out the yearly tithes that should be gotten from the food produced. If there are fruits in blossom before this day, the fruits belong to the year before. All fruits that blossom on that day or a day later are New Year fruits. On this day, you're going to celebrate by munching on some delicious olives, figs, dates, and of course, pomegranates. These are the specific foods mentioned in the Torah that you must consume. When you taste these fruits for the first time in the year, you have to give blessings.

Purim falls on the 14th day of the month of Adar, which could fall in February or March. What's significant about this event is that the Jews were rescued from Haman, the terrible Persian prime minister. You'll enjoy not just the retelling of the rescue but plays and kindness from others. On this day, you have the se'udat Purim to look forward to as well. You'll also enjoy the various attires and masks that people adorn themselves with and lovely little cookies as well.

Pesach is the Passover, a celebration of the escape of the Israelites from Egypt. This begins on the 15th day of Nisan, which usually falls in March or April. It's a well-known and loved Jewish holy day. Israelites and Reform Jews celebrate Pesach for seven days, and for conservative and orthodox Jews, the celebrations last for eight days. The eves of the first and second days are kicked off with ritual meals known as Seders. The Seders are accompanied by retelling the Passover story and eating foods that are symbolic. In the Book of Exodus, the Egyptians suffered ten plagues from God because they refused to listen to heed his command to let his people go. Right before God was about to unleash the worst of the plagues he had in store for the Egyptians, where every firstborn son born to an Egyptian family would die, God told the Israelites they had to have a special marking on their doorposts so that they wouldn't lose their own firstborn sons. The marking was to be made with the blood of a lamb. This blood kept them safe as the destroying spirit of the Lord went about reaping the souls of the firstborn Egyptian sons. After the plague, Pharaoh finally gave in and asked Moses and Aaron to get out of Egypt with their people.

Yom HaShoah happens on the 27th day of Nisan. Some call it Holocaust Remembrance Day. This holy day comes a week after the final day of Pesach. Shoah is a Hebrew word that means "utter destruction" and is about the genocide of the Jews in World War II. This day is meant to honor the memories of the millions whose lives were stolen in the Shoah.

Shavuot means "weeks," and it's held over two days. Shavuot is a Jewish holiday celebrated on the religious festival of the same name. It falls on the seventh day of the Hebrew month of Sivan. This unique holiday celebrates God giving Torah to Israel, and there are many customs associated with this celebration in Judaism. It is believed that Shavuot marks humanity's first step towards learning to be master over nature and its blessings. This is celebrated as we retell the events of the Exodus from Egypt and also celebrate God's delivery of the Torah to Israel. The Torah portion read on this day is Bamidbar. During the month of Sivan, you fast for 20 days in preparation for the celebration of Shavuot. The last four days of these are called "Sh'vaot" (or "Shavuot"). The Festival of Shavuot is a three-day celebration, the first day being the most important. On this day, a person must not eat or drink anything that may cause them to become impure. What is prohibited on Shavuot include, but are not limited to: sexual activity, bathing in a mikvah (ritual bath), and eating fruits and vegetables before they have been harvested. The second day of Shavuot is also known as the "Kiddush" day. The Kiddush is a blessing that celebrates the giving of the Torah to the Jewish people. This blessing takes place on this day, and only on this day, before eating anything that may cause the celebrant to become impure, one must say: "May the Lord open my lips, and my mouth shall proclaim Your praise, all day long." One can recite both parts of this blessing in Hebrew or Yiddish. The third day, Sukkot, is a holiday all to itself. This means that those who celebrate Sukkot will not do so on the third day of Shavuot. However, if someone did not celebrate Sukkot during the last month of Tishrei, they are allowed to observe it now. This is declared as such because it celebrates that the Jewish people were freed from oppression in Egypt and were finally able to enter their Promised Land.

Tisha B'Av is the ninth day of the month of Av, and it is a Jewish fast day commemorating the destruction of both Temples in Jerusalem. Its name is derived from Isaiah (59:1) and Jeremiah (2:36), which predicted that the Babylonian and Persian Empires would solemnize this day as a fast. Jews all over the world are encouraged to commemorate, observe, and mourn these tragedies with prayers, fasting, and other rituals. The First Temple was destroyed by the Babylonians under the leadership of Nebuchadnezzar II, in 586 BCE, in what is referred to as the Babylonian Captivity. This was a particularly traumatic time for the Jewish people due to the loss of their nation and temple. Jews who were exiled to Babylon were among those who began observing Tisha B'Av when they returned home after Cyrus permitted them to end their exile. The Second Temple was destroyed in 70 CE by the Romans, led by Titus. This was a much more devastating event for the Jewish people since it resulted in the loss of their homeland and further exile. From then on,

Tisha B'Av became a day of mourning for the destruction that visited upon both Temples as well as other tragedies, such as foreign conquest and persecution, which have befallen Jews over the course of history.

Chapter Nine: Kashrut and Other Kosher Foods

Jewish mysticism holds that kosher food is food that's healthy for the soul. If you're going to practice Jewish magic easily, you need to keep your soul nourished with the right food because eating is seen as a purification process by the Kabbalah. According to Jewish law, food contains Divine energy, which implies that eating the right meals could help you become more attuned to spiritual matters.

What Is Kashrut?

Kashrut is also known as Jewish dietary law. Kosher foods are those that are in accordance with Jewish dietary laws, which were established to keep kosher animals and to reduce the amount of fat in meat. Kosher is "fit and suitable" or "proper," according to Webster's. Orthodox Jews strictly follow these dietary laws, preparing food for themselves without non-kosher ingredients in the kitchen.

The world over, people are interested in what kosher means, especially why it is so important to the Jewish faith. As with many other religions, Judaism has strict rules concerning food. Although these rules differ from religion to religion, they can be considered some of the basic characteristics of what a kosher diet entails. Using natural and organic ingredients is generally recommended, as is eating less meat and dairy products and more fish, fruits, vegetables, and grains. It also means you can't eat blood from mammals or poultry, nor can you combine meat and milk. There are also things you must not do in the kitchen. Those who want to observe all or some of the rules simply do so to remember their roots.

Many explanations have been given for the different aspects of Kashrut. The Torah tells devotees that to have a good level of holiness, they'll need certain restrictions around food that would set them apart from others. Some explanations are rooted in the different classes of behavior based on Judaism, such as being kind to animals and avoiding animal cruelty. There are also explanations offered by experts that come about from comparing various religions. There's no explanation yet that satisfies everyone, but many of them have helped help Jews observe the restrictions, even when challenging.

Kashrut is rooted in the Torah. It helps you know which animals are fine to eat and that you shouldn't cook a goat's kid In the mil of its mother, among other specific things. The laws keeping you from eating are meant to act as a way to help you be more in alignment with the Torah, and, ultimately, with God. For most modern-day Jews and modern movements, the Kashrut is a matter that can be followed to the extent that the faithful deems appropriate.

Kosher Food

Not every animal or meal is kosher, and you also have to think about whether the animal you're about to eat was healthy and how it was killed. If it wasn't killed humanely, you shouldn't be eating it. You also shouldn't be eating blood, so to avoid that, make sure to soak your meat in salt water. If your fish has scales and fins, it's okay to eat it, but you don't have to worry about any special preparation technique. Not sure about what you're eating? No worries. Several regulatory bodies are in place to check that your food is certified kosher, and when that's the case, there's a symbol on the pack to let you know it's safe.

Eating kosher means combining meat and milk is a no-no, and yes, *that includes pizza.* You have to think about the different ways these combinations can show up in meals so you avoid breaking the rules. Also, you may need to have different plates, pots, pans, and so on for meat and dairy so that there's no cross-contamination. There are some homes where you'll find items that aren't used for either. Kitchenware you don't use for either meat or milk is considered *Pareve*, and if you're using those tools, you can either make meals of meat or dairy. Your kitchen has to be kosher, but don't let that scare you; working within the rules is not as hard as it seems.

Kosher Animals

Does the animal you're about to eat chew the cud? Are its hooves split? Then it's okay to eat it. Among the safe animals are deer, sheep, and cows. The rabbit, horse, and pig are the exceptions to this rule. The slaughter of these animals must comply with *Shechita,* which the Torah describes in detail. It's the fastest way to kill an animal and hurts the least. The slaughter is usually done by a Shochet, who is well-versed in the Shechita laws.

Among the meat that is considered to be Kosher are deer, sheep, and cow's meat.
https://unsplash.com/photos/YlAmh_X_SsE

All fat, meat, and other things from an animal slaughtered in a way that doesn't respect Shechita are not kosher. Any biscuit, cake, or confectionery made with animal fat isn't kosher. All foods that are produced with animal derivatives need to be kosher. After an animal is slaughtered, the Shochet has to check it to ensure no defects. When there is a defect, the animal is *treifa*, which means "torn." The animal is, therefore, not kosher. Usually, the defects are seen in the animal's lungs. Healthy, smooth lungs mean they are Glatt. All non-kosher things are treifa. Regarding birds, the Torah declared that 24 species aren't good for eating, including every bird of prey. You may have turkey, duck, goose, and chicken.

Salted Meat

It's not enough to make sure that a Shochet slaughters the poultry and animals. The Torah explains that getting rid of all the blood from the slaughtered animal is important, which can be done through salting. First, the meat is washed thoroughly and soaked for half an hour in water. After this, the meat is drained on a slanting board and then sprinkled with salt (the medium coarse kind). This way, any residual blood is forced out of the meat. You must ensure the salt is sprinkled on every side. Also, don't skip the cuts and folds in the meat. Let the meat sit on the slanting board for an hour so all the blood can clear out. After this, the meat is rinsed under running water, completely removing the blood. When you're done, the meat is fit to cook and eat. It's obvious why you may not want to buy your meat or poultry from a non-kosher store because even if the animal the meat is from a kosher animal, someone other than a Shochet slaughtered it, which means its meat isn't kosher. Also, the odds are the salting process isn't common outside of Jewish spaces. However, you can buy already packed fowl and meat with a Hensher. This symbol is a kosher one, a stamp signifying the food has had Rabbinical supervision. Rabbinical supervision is when ingredients are checked by a group of Rabbis, who ensure that the ingredients are certified kosher. Usually, this sign will say Kosher Lemehadrin, meaning the product is extremely kosher, which is helpful for those who lean orthodox or conservative in their practice.

Certain parts of the meat in question may have too much blood to be salted enough to get rid of it all, and this is the case with the liver. To eat liver, it should be roasted with an open flame as this is the only way to drain the blood. Some veins and fats, in particular, have to be removed before eating, and the process is known as *Nikkur*. The duties of a kosher butcher, therefore, include:

- Ensuring to only slaughter kosher animals that chew the cud and have split hoofs, as well as kosher poultry
- Slaughtering the animal

- Checking the slaughtered animal for any defects
- Removing the veins and fats
- Roasting liver
- Salting meat.

The butcher and Shochet have to be practicing Jews, and the safest place to buy meat from as a Jew is from a butcher who has a kashrut certificate from a proper Beth Din, which is the Jewish Law Court. Note that shellfish, eels, prawns, and crabs aren't kosher. If there's ever any doubt about what's kosher and what isn't, you should check in with your Rabbi.

Milk

Milk is considered kosher when the source is kosher, too. So it's fine to have goat and cow milk, but you can't have horse or pig milk. These days, there are regulations to ensure that dairy farms are up to code. However, you can be certain that farmers aren't adding non-kosher milk to your regular milk. Still, for most Orthodox Jews, it is important to only have supervised milk — milk inspected by a mashgiach who ensures that bottled milk is strictly kosher. This milk is known as Cholov Yisrael. Cheese must be from a kosher animal, and in the preparation process, you must be sure the rennets are also from a kosher animal. This is hardly the case with commercially made cheese, so it's best to look for cheese with Rabbinical supervision. On the topic of meat and milk, you have to wait six hours after eating meat before you can have anything with milk in it. You should wait three or six hours before eating meat when you've eaten hard cheese. For soft cheese, yogurt, milk, and lighter dairy products, you can wait an hour or half an hour to enjoy your meat.

Veggies and Fruits

Generally, fruits and veggies are kosher. Note that it's not okay to eat fruit if it happens to be part of the yield from the first three years of the tree's existence. Those fruits are known as *Orlah*. If the fruits are from Israel, they must be tithed — this is Hafrashat Terumah Umaaser. During tithe, there's the recital of a special text. Every seven years, Shmittah is held in Israel. Think of it as a Sabbatical year, when there are specific laws regarding veggies and fruits in Israel all through that time. It's not uncommon to find insect-infested veggies and fruits at this time. The Torah is clear about not eating insects, which means you have to inspect your foods for insects — especially those likely to be infested, like dates, lettuce, etc. The inspection is known as Bedikat Tolaim.

Eggs

It's only fine to have eggs that are from kosher poultry. Often, kosher eggs have a pointed end and a round one, but non-kosher eggs are often round all the way. You need to check the eggs to ensure there are no blood clots and throw away the ones with a clot.

Tevilat Kelim

Any item made of glass or metal in the kitchen has to go into a mikvah before you can use it. The same goes for glazed earthenware. Immersing your utensils is called Tevilat kelim, which means "immersion of vessels." Before the immersion, a special blessing is said.

Parev and Wine

Parev literally means neither meat nor milk. Since veggies are considered parev, you can enjoy them with either milk or meat. Everyone has to check if they are milchig (they've consumed milk), fleishig (they've consumed meat), or Parev. For instance, if you had chicken for dinner at 6 PM, you can't enjoy a glass of milk at 8 PM because you're *fleishig* or meaty. When it comes to fish and milk, you're not supposed to cook them together, but you can eat them one after the other right away. You can also have meat and fish together. As for wine, you can only have it under Rabbinical supervision, and the wine should have a Hechsher on it.

Bread

The thing about bread is that most have animal fat or have come in contact with it somehow. Therefore, whatever bread you want to eat, the bakery needs to have been checked to ensure every ingredient is kosher. This is why many Jews will only eat bread made by another Jew. This bread is called *Pas Yisrael*. Jewish bakers who make their own Challah need to set aside a piece of dough in a process called "the separation of

Challah" before they bake the bread. Traditionally, that separated piece is offered to a kohen, but now it is simply burned and disposed of properly. There's a special blessing to be said as you separate the Challah, a task that is commanded and often done by women.

Why Kashrut Matters

The Torah has issued explicit instructions on Kashrut, but it gives no clear reason why it's important. Therefore, you can think of Kashrut in one of three ways to motivate you to stick with it. First, all humans are the creation of God. Since God is the grand architect, he should definitely know what would work best for everyone so that all needs can be met, whether those needs are spiritual, mental, or physical. It only makes sense to follow the instructions of the manufacturer of a machine so you can operate the machine efficiently and safely. The same applies when it comes to God and humans. God knows that for the Jews, non-kosher food is terrible. You can, therefore, trust that God's instructions about these meals are for your own good.

Another thing to consider is that you may give your reasons for following Kashrut. For instance, you can realize that you're what you eat, so if you only eat the domesticated, kosher animals, you're likely to take on their good energy and character through the food. Eating wild animals could give you much wilder traits that may not serve you, and also, kosher animals are generally cleaner than the others.

One final point to consider is that you're walking the path of Judaism because you want to return to God, to be so close to him that you might as well be one with him. Therefore, it only makes sense that you should keep his words and abide by his laws so that you, too, can become holy as he is. Also, it makes it very clear that you are God's chosen person. When you doubt what to eat, you can get a Kashrut list from your Rabbi, so there's no doubt in your mind that you're keeping kosher.

Chapter Ten: Jewish Meditation and Prayer

As you already know, Hebrew is a divine language. Do you know that each letter of the Hebrew alphabet carries a certain energy you can meditate on? This chapter will teach you all you need to know about working magically with the Hebrew alphabet.

The Power of Hebrew Letters

Jewish tradition holds that the world exists because God spoke it into being. The word of God drives all of creation. Each letter of the sacred language of God acts as a carrier of spirit and life. The Hebrew alphabet is the reason the world continues to turn. These letters have literal meanings as well as deeper, mystical meanings. When you understand each of them, you can glean the hidden mysteries in the Torah and life in general. Studying these letters may cause you to sense a deep connection to spirit that you can't express with ordinary words. Kabbalists are known to meditate on the letters to get a better sense of them and their transformational power. You should take the time to study these letters if you want an even deeper, richer spiritual experience. Know that this chapter is only a starting point and that the practice of studying these letters should ideally be a lifelong matter.

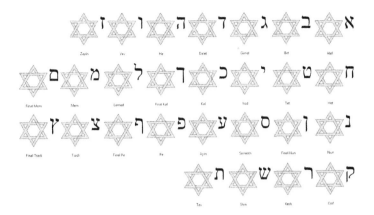

The Hebrew alphabet.

Icatflower, CC BY-SA 4.0 <https://creativecommons.org/licenses/by-sa/4.0>, via Wikimedia Commons https://commons.wikimedia.org/wiki/File:Magen_David_Hebrew_Alphabet.png

Aleph

This is the first letter of the Hebrew alphabet. It represents number one and the idea of Oneness. It's about achieving Unity with the Divine, and its energy reminds the faithful that everything is one and the same despite the seeming duality of all things. Aleph is a reminder that all things come from the same source and are the same thing, even though they seem separate. It is about the omnipresent, spaceless, timeless existence that can't be divided and that which is perfect beyond understanding.

Beith

The second letter of the Hebrew alphabet, Beith, represents the number and energy of two. As the first letter in the creation story, it represents beginning of duality of Creator/creation – a creation which gives and which receives. Think of Beith as a quantum jump from Unity to duality, allowing for opposites to exist. This letter literally refers to a house, representing the idea of being a vessel or a container. That which is created houses within it the power of the Creator. The physical world serves as a vessel to express God's glory.

In the same way, the physical body acts as the container of the soul. It's the soul that drives the body's being in the world. The dual world still has Unity within it, but the Unity is hidden. Beith is the very root of all buildings, as it contains and then births the letters to come.

Gimel

The third letter represents the idea of harmonizing or balancing out opposites. Gimel acts as a connector between Aleph and Beith, bringing balance to both energies. It's a letter representing the concept of constant change, movement, and transformation, and it literally means "camel." The camel is an animal used to transport people and things, so the Gimel has to do with travel and constant motion. It is the embodiment of both reward and punishment, giving and receiving so that there's always a balance between two things that oppose each other. It also represents the ideas of cultivation, kindness, nurturing, and helping things grow. It's a sign that the Creator is ever generous and benevolent to the created, offering abundant prosperity and life. Gimel represents the idea that blessings flow to those who conduct themselves in a good way while acting unjustly leads to blockages in abundance and goodness.

Dallet

This letter means "door" or "gate," representing the selfless state of being and humility required to go through the doors of your mystery to return to the power of the One or Aleph. Dallet is like a man bent over, representing the idea of being receptive and humble. It's about the structure you need before receiving the good, representing the idea of remaining diligent till you've been blessed.

Sometimes, Dallet is thought of as Dalit, a poor man who has been blessed thanks to the Creator's generosity, as shown by Gimel. It's the awareness that humans have nothing that's truly theirs, as all their wants and needs are fulfilled thanks to the Creator. Even your breath and ability to move are from him and no one else. Dallet is also about structure. Looking at the letter, it looks a bit like a step on a staircase, which you climb figuratively to overcome resistance to study and growth in your practice. If this letter is in your name, it signifies strengths like diligence band the ability to organize, plan, and build.

Hei

The fifth letter of the Hebrew alphabet's fifth letter, it embodies divine revelation. It is God's breath by which he made all of heaven and earth. The word was created as soon as God uttered Hei. This letter represents the idea of life as a gift, and it's that which spells the verb "to be" or Haya, meaning "being." Hei is divinity, the spiritual outcome of life that comes through the previous letters. This letter represents the essence of life within all created things and beings, and it is the idea of effortlessness in how the world continues to turn. It is also about the concepts of specificity, gentleness, and divinity. It's also a representation of the freedom of choice. You can find this letter in the holy name, making it very special among the Aleph-Beith.

Vav

Vav translates to "peg" or "hook," and it is depicted as a simple vertical line, serving a a sort of symbol of the outward projection of God's perfection. This projection is over and within all things created by God, and it makes it possible for him to rule over the affairs of his creation. It's thanks to this projection that the various cycles in life continue unbroken so that mankind can thrive and develop until it's time for God's Oneness and Unity to be revealed to and within everyone. Think of Vav as a sort of hose, allowing a flow of shefa (abundance) from God above to his creations below. It's Jacob's ladder, planted firmly in the ground on earth, with its top in the heavens. It's also seen as Yod's extension, which is where all creation has its origin. The Vav is a lesson on being present, a requirement to connect your physical and spiritual lives. This letter also stands for the number 6, the 6 days of creation, and the 6 physical directions. The physical directions are left and right, up and down, and front and back. The letter is also a phallic symbol meant to bring life, continuity, fertility, and abundance. It is the energy of that which adds.

Zayin

Zayin appears similar to a sword and reminds us of concepts like struggle, sustenance, and spirit. Being the seventh letter, it also represents the idea of Shabbat, the day on which you're meant to rest and tend to your spiritual affairs. From Zayin comes all movement, and it is impregnating energy that causes creation to move. It looks like a Vav but with a crown on it. It is about the struggle between opposites, the fight for existence, and the battle for sustenance.

Heith

This is the letter of infinite possibilities. Think of it like a doorway that turns, allowing you access to higher levels of life in the spirit. It lets you go deep into your soul's mysteries and return to normal waking consciousness. The letter resembles a ladder, showing you that you can break through limitations, which makes sense since it represents the energy of 8, which involves transcending the natural course of things. It's also the embodiment of wisdom.

Teith

Teith means "nest" or "basket" and represents the inherent good in all created. The Teith is a picture of a serpent coiled around a stick. The serpent is the embodiment of the wisdom and knowledge of the serpent in the garden of Eden. The serpent is also a symbol of the healing of the soul, the serpent was lifted up by Moses in the wilderness and whoever looked upon it was healed. The serpent is also a symbol of kundalini energy which rises through the chakras and activates spiritual awareness. The serpent also represents the serpent in the book of revelation that surrounds the throne of God.

Additionally, the letter Teith is associated with the word "tov" (good) and the concept of "goodness" or "virtue."

It is said that the one who meditates on the letter Teith will gain wisdom, understanding, and knowledge. It also represents the power of the spoken word and its ability to bring healing and revelation.

Yod

The tenth letter of the alphabet is a simple point or dot that represents God, from which all things created emerge. It represents Unity even within seeming multiplicity. This is the root of all roots, the Divine Spark that lies hidden within all. This is the spark that causes all things to exist. It's the power of spirit over matter. Yod represents the Creator, whose name starts with this letter.

In the same way, many things happen in the world, but they are all from the one source, that which is indivisible and perfect beyond comprehension. This letter also represents the ten emanations. All things come from Yod and shall return to Yod. It represents that which is beyond space, time, and thought, unperceivable and in one and all.

Khaf

The eleventh letter refers to the cupped palm of a hand stretched out to receive. The shape of the letter is reminiscent of a container, whether a jar or cup. It can be used to receive. As a building houses what happens with the people within it, so does the body act as a house for the energy and life force that animate it. The Khaf is a lesson to shape yourself. Its lessons include humility, letting go of that which causes resistance, bending matter to the will of spirit, and spirit to matter. It's about wise thoughts being put into action to receive concrete results and manifestations. The letter asks you to consider what you constantly contain and change it to attain the preferred reality you want.

Lammed

This letter is a sign of learning and the word for a goad or staff. You can find it in the middle of the Aleph-Beith, so it makes sense that it represents the heart. To learn in Kabbalah, one must do so with heart and soul, for it's not enough to focus only on the mind. The letter shows that spiritual learning is critical to human existence and that everyone is here to learn and express their spiritual lessons through practice in the physical world. When you've dealt with your non-beneficial traits in Khaf, and your ego isn't big enough to interfere any longer, you can learn the perfection of your spirit, master God's laws, and understand his ways so you can live in alignment with him.

Mem

This thirteenth letter represents the Torah and the waters of knowledge and wisdom. It's about manifestation and being willing and able to sink your teeth into the wisdom available to you. It is believed that everyone hungers for God's words, which are life's waters. It's also a representation of the fact that before things can come to fruition, they need time to blossom, and therefore it is important to keep emotions in check and remain humble. This letter matches the energy of the number 40, representing the time required for things to come to fruition. For instance, the embryo needs 40 days to develop fully, the Israelites spent 40 years in the desert before they finally arrived at the holy land they were promised, and Moses needed 40 years to develop and be ready to be Israel's leader.

Nuun

This letter represents faithfulness, the soul, and the idea of something emerging, continuity, fertility, increase, multiplication, and humility because it bends at the top and bottom. Some consider it a symbol for the 50 Gates of Wisdom of Binah. Nuun is about remaining present and how the soul stays humble, silently offering its light but remaining in the shadows. Nuun is an illustration that to follow the Creator's will rather than your own ego, you need to bend above and below. This letter also demonstrates the relationship between the impermanent body and the permanent soul. In Aramaic, it means "fish." So, the letter is a lesson on how to flow and remain flexible like fish when it comes to change.

Samekh

Samekh represents memory, protection, and support. The circumference of the letter shows God, while the inner part is God's creation, whom he keeps safe and supporting in all they do. The letter represents the Ohr Makif, the Surrounding Light of Kabbalah, a representation of God's providence that continues to encompass and drive all of existence. Samekh is that which contains the form of all things. It's a lesson on circular thinking, asking you not to think only for yourself but for the good of everyone. This is the process of thinking with your soul and being inclusive, as you learn each day that wisdom doesn't just lie in one container but is in everyone. The Samekh is a lesson that to know God, you must let go of the self-imposed limitations on your mind. You've got to drop everything you think you know about how life works and dare to disregard the physical world and its limitations so that you can know who you really are. When you can cleanse yourself of negativity and limited thinking, master your ego, stay humble, and keep your ears open to the voice of your soul, it's worth it. You will find you're always supported, protected, and helped at every turn. Nun combined with Samekh is Nes, and this means "miracle." Knowing the lessons Nuun and Samekh have for you, you can discover and make miracles happen.

Ayin

This letter means "eye, "so it involves vision and revealing previously hidden lights. Ayin asks you to look beyond, and it is also about time. It's about being a visionary. You've got to keep your focus on the present as well as the future. The proper pronunciation of the word Ayin gives a guttural sound that activates the thyroid gland. Ayin is a part of many words that have to do with the concept of time. Some of these words are:

- Eternity
- Till
- Moment
- Past
- Future

- Hours
- Time

Ayin is a lesson that teaches that you need to understand cause and effect and how your present choices and decisions can affect the results you get in the future. It asks you to keep your eyes open and see beyond what is physical as its energy takes you from the darkness into light. It's about seeing through the darkness of limitations to the good that isn't visible yet.

Peh

Peh is a letter that means "mouth." The Kabbalah considers speed to be a spiritual ability that can be used to give life or cause death. You are what you think, and what you think is what you speak, meaning your words can give you a new reality. The quality of your speech is a mirror of the quality of life you live. Peh is a lesson on choosing your words wisely and not wasting them creating situations you don't really want.

There's a quote from the Talmud Baba Messiah that says, "Don't say one thing with the mouth and another with the heart." This is the lesson Peh teaches all. Use your words to speak your destiny into being. Awaken your spirit with the right thoughts and proper speech.

Tsadde

Like other Hebrew letters, the Tsadde is also associated with certain meanings and interpretations. The Tsadde is formed by two Hebrew letters, 'zayin' and 'dalet' which resemble a fishhook, this shape can be connected with the word "tsadik" (righteous) or the concept of "righteousness." A fishhook is also a symbol of something that catches and holds on, in this way it represents the ability to hold on to righteousness and maintain it.

Additionally, the letter Tsadde is associated with the word "tzaddik" (a righteous person) and the concept of "righteousness" or "justice." It is said that the one who meditates on the letter Tsadde will gain righteousness, justice and the ability to hold on to righteousness.

It is also the letter of the Zohar, the book of splendor, which teaches the secrets of the creation of the universe and the human soul. It is said that the one who studies the Zohar will gain wisdom and understanding of the spiritual dimension.

Khof

This letter is called Qof or Kuf. It may refer to a needle's eye, as well as the back of one's head. Khof is also a word for "monkey," representing the sacred and profane (Kedushah and Klipah). The husk or peel represents all the negativity in this created world. Khof is about needing to take this peel or hist away to show what is holy and lies within you. As Khof means "monkey," it also represents the human who hasn't mastered their base instincts and is still animalistic, with no higher thinking faculties. This letter is a call to rise above the animalistic tendencies in humans so that they can be more like God. Khof is the one letter in the Aleph-Beith that stretches below the other letter's line, which represents the idea of going into the lower world and the chance to ride from there. Kuf also means circle, which is about nature's many cycles. It's a reminder that your life has cycles, and you must change and evolve to uncover your full spiritual light.

Reish

It is said that the Reish represents the head, as it is the first letter of the word "rosh" (head). This meaning can be connected to the idea of leadership and authority.

Additionally, the letter Reish is associated with the word "rachamim" (mercy) and the concept of "mercy" or "compassion." It is said that the one who meditates on the letter Reish will gain compassion and mercy, and will be able to extend compassion to others.

The word "Reish" also has several meanings in Hebrew, depending on the context. Some of the most common meanings include "head," "leader," "boss," "chief," "prince," "ruler," and "first." In some biblical texts, "reish" also refers to the beginning or the top of something.

It is also the letter of the God's name El-Roi, the God who sees, and the letter of the word Rabbi, which means teacher or master.

You can break through challenges, break things down into their smallest units, and build something new from scraps. Reish is also connected to the Reshimo, representing the spiritual DNA everyone is meant to express and discover in life. Within Reish are the secrets of the beginning or Beresheet. The letter also represents the secrets contained in Keter, the highest of all Sephirot.

Shin

Shin is about transformation and fire. The Shin is formed by three Hebrew letters, which resemble the shape of a tooth and it is the first letter of the word "shinayim" (two) and "shalom" (peace)

Additionally, the letter Shin is associated with the word "shaddai" (Almighty) and the concept of "Almighty" or "all-powerful." It is said that the one who meditates on the letter Shin will gain the power of the divine, and the ability to manifest their desires.

It is also the letter of the word "shamayim" (heavens) and the letter of the name of God as "Shaddai" (Almighty) and also the letter of the word "Shekinah" (The presence of God).

The Shin has a special significance in Kabbalah, where it is believed to represent the three sefirot of wisdom, understanding, and knowledge. It is also associated with the element of fire, which is often associated with God's presence, and is often used to represent the divine spark within each individual.

Tav

The last letter of the Aleph-Beith, this one means "seal," "omen," "sign," or "mark." It represents the idea of completion. It's also about perfection, truth, and the Tikkun's respiration. It's a call to come back to your life's purpose, complete it, and start over with Aleph's Oneness. The Tav is a revelation that even from the beginning, there was an end waiting to be experienced. It's the last letters of the Beresheet, too. This letter teaches that all things were put in place by God to get one and all to a final level of being perfect. This is where all creation can be truly fulfilled. It's the completion of the real truth. As soon as Tav has been accomplished, one has no choice but to go back to Aleph, as all life is a cycle. Aleph is the source of all things and the beginning. Tav is never actually the end but the start of new things.

How to Meditate on Hebrew Letters

Contemplating these letters offers you a connection to God and his power, which you can use to change your life for the better. Here's a simple exercise to meditate on any letter you want:

1. First, look at the letter. Do this for five minutes, studying its form. You're practicing "engraving" or chakikah, which will help you see the letter so clearly that it doesn't move or waver when you envision it.

2. Shut your eyes and bring the image of the letter to your mind's eye. Initially, it might be a bit of a struggle, but don't let that stop you. With time, you'll be able to hold the image in your mind for longer.

3. If you notice other images in your mind's eye, that's fine. Just focus on the letter until that's all on your mind. This process of removing the other images by focusing on the letter is called chatzivah or hewing.

4. Let the image sit in your mind for fifteen minutes. If you need to remind yourself of what you're supposed to be seeing, you can open your eyes to take in the image and then go back to see it in your mind's eye. If you're still struggling with other images in your mind, see the letter a being black against a white background and cut out other things around it. Take your time with this. With each practice, you'll get better.

It is important to note that you shouldn't concern yourself with the results of this meditation. Do this daily for thirty days, and you'll be amazed at the results.

Prayers for Sephiroth

Note that you can make these prayers as long or as short as you want, and you can simply repeat a phrase over and over if you prefer, contemplating the meaning of what you're saying.

Keter: Ask God to connect you with the spiritual realms and thank him for doing so.

Chochmah: Ask God to grant you the wisdom you need to achieve your vision.

Binah: Ask God to give you deep understanding. You can contemplate the Binah when you're dealing with a matter that has you confused or when you want more light about what a certain portion of the Torah means to you.

Chesed: Ask the Creator to show you how to be benevolent and kind as he is.

Gevurah: Seek the Divine's help with his power so you can change things in your life. Alternatively, you can pray for the ability to exercise restraint.

Tiferet: You can ask God to show you the beauty and harmony in the worst of situations, or in yourself, or in someone else.

Netzach: Ask God to manifest himself triumphantly in whatever situation you find yourself in. You can also pray for endurance to go through life.

Hod: You can pray for God's glory to be evident in your life or ask that you have a life where you can hold your head high in dignity.

Yesod: While focusing on this sefirah, ask God to help you live a righteous life so you have a solid foundation to build your relationship with him.

Malchut: You can pray to God to make his presence unmistakable in your life so that your life is one full of miracles, mercy, kindness, love, blessings, and abundance.

Extra: Jewish Terms You Should Know

Many terms in Hebrew underscore important aspects of Jewish mysticism. You should know what they are so that you can work with them with understanding.

Hebrew – The language spoken by Jews. The Hebrew language was originally written in square Hebrew characters, but through the years has later developed into a more common alphabet. Throughout its long history, changes have been made to the alphabet and its various forms of punctuation and script.

Qabalah - This is the name given to a form of Jewish mysticism that is based on the concept of creation. Qabalah goes into detail regarding the nature of God and what it is that He created, which in turn, helps us understand ourselves.

Torah - This is the word used in the Jewish language to refer to the first five books of the Bible. The Torah begins with Genesis and ends with Deuteronomy. Originally, it was not called the "Talmud" until it was later combined with the Talmud into a single book.

Tanakh - This is the name given to the Jewish Bible. Tanakh means "The Law or Teaching" in Hebrew. It consists of three main divisions: Torah, Nevi'im, and Ketuvim. These three main divisions are further subdivided into the various books that make up these divisions.

Mishnah - This is a collection of Judaism's Oral Laws, which were created around 200 CE by Rabbi Judah HaNasi and his colleagues after they codified the oral tradition of the Torah. These laws were based on scripture but also included some statements concerning how Israel should live during their period.

Tzitzit - Is another Hebrew word for "fringes."

Halakha - Is the Jewish Law. Jewish laws help define many things in Judaism, such as a proper Sabbath meal and how it should be prepared.

Challah - Is a type of bread that is made without yeast. Its name comes from the Old French word "Lacaille," which came from the Latin "Laicola" and means "loaf." This bread contains eggs, sugar, oil or butter, and water.

Chumash - This is another Hebrew word for "five," which in the Jewish faith is used to describe the five books of the Torah.

Halachot - This is another Hebrew word used to describe Jewish laws.

Kosher - This means "fit" or "proper." Today, kosher is often associated with dietary laws that are set by Judaism and followed by religious Jews. To be considered Kosher, food must be prepared according to specific rules and regulations. Kosher comes from the Hebrew term for fit and proper, "kasher."

Shabbat - Is another Hebrew word for Sabbath. Shabbat is a part of the Jewish faith and observance of God's laws. It is a day that all Jews are encouraged to keep as close to their religious beliefs as possible.

Rosh Hashanah - Is the Festival of Trumpets or New Year. The name refers directly to the sound that is heard on this day. Expect the Festival of Trumpets at the end of September.

Yom Kippur - Is the Day of Repentance. This holiday occurs in mid-September and is a very solemn, holy time for Jews, where they fast and pray for their sins committed throughout their yearlong lives.

Chassidic - This is a term used to describe a group of orthodox Jewish sects and traditions. The first use of the word "Chassidism" can be traced back to the Eastern European Jews in the 18th century. These Chassidic groups were typically known for their long beards and dark clothing.

Yeshiva - This is another Hebrew word that is used to describe an academy or college dedicated to studying Torah and other religious writings, such as Chassidic literature. Yeshivas are typically located in Israel, attracting men who want to become rabbis and Jewish teachers.

Rabbi – This is another Hebrew word for Rabbi. It is often used in comparison with "Reb" or "Rabbi" to describe someone more learned or better qualified than the other person. Today it is a widely used term, particularly by Jews and non-Jews.

Pesach – Is another Hebrew word that means Passover or Passover Festival. It refers to the celebration of the liberation of the Israelites from slavery in Egypt. This festival gives Jews a chance to reflect on their freedom and thank God for it by eating matzo, a holy food.

Chavurah – Is another Hebrew word that has been used to describe a group of Jews who are collectively bonded by their faith. Today, the word is less commonly used than in previous generations and is typically reserved for the most closely knit of Jewish communities.

Shalom – In Hebrew, Shalom means peace, but it can also be used positively to describe people who are kind and want to help others. The word is sometimes misused today to refer to non-Jews or non-Jewish activities.

Mitzvah - This is an alternative spelling of the word Mitzvot, another Hebrew word for commandment. In Judaism, this refers to a specific religious rule that Jews must follow.

Matzo – Is an unleavened bread that is eaten on Passover. It is made with flour and water and baked in a very hot oven that kills all of the yeast, which would make it rise. Matzo can also be used as a way to replace leavening during other Jewish holidays or funerals as well.

Bar Mitzvah - It is the term that is typically used to describe a Jewish boy who is becoming a man. This ceremony is on his 13th birthday as a symbol of his entrance into adulthood in the eyes of God.

Bat Mitzvah - It is the term that is typically used to describe a Jewish girl who is becoming a woman. This ceremony is on her 12th birthday, and it marks the entrance of young womanhood into the life of God.

Kiddush - This prayer is for all Jews. They recite to praise God and show their thankfulness for His many blessings. The prayer is recited before every meal.

Kashrut - This is another Hebrew word that refers to the laws and rules of keeping kosher food, which is set forth by Judaism and followed by religious Jews and other people who follow Jewish traditions.

Teshuvah - Is a Hebrew word that refers to repentance and is used in the Jewish faith to describe spiritual reforms and conversions.

Beit Din - Is another Hebrew word for religious court. In Judaism, Beit Dins are courts established to judge disputes between Jews living in Judea during the era of Jesus' birth and death or with other Jews or non-Jews when there are criminal or civil issues involved.

B'nai Mitzvah – This is a Hebrew word that refers to a Jewish person who is learning about Jewish law, though it can also be used to describe a Jewish girl who is becoming a woman. This ceremony marks the entrance of young womanhood into the life of God by celebrating her transition from childhood to womanhood.

Tallit - This Hebrew word refers to a prayer shawl worn by Orthodox Jews. It is also referred to as a tallit katan or a "prayer scarf." This cloth was traditionally made out of wool, but it can be made from other materials today.

Tefillin - This is another term for tefillin, which are small black boxes that have been used for centuries to hold Jewish scriptures. They contain verses from the Torah and are customarily worn by both men and women on their arms and heads during morning prayers.

Kippah - This is another Hebrew word that describes a Jewish skullcap worn by all Orthodox Jews.

List of Hebrew Letters

1. Aleph
2. Beith
3. Gimel
4. Dallet
5. Hei
6. Vav
7. Zayin
8. Heith
9. Teith
10. Yod
11. Khaf

12. Lammed
13. Mem
14. Nuun
15. Samekh
16. Ayin
17. Peh
18. Tsadde
19. Khof
20. Reish
21. Shin
22. Tav

Here's another book by Silvia Hill that you might like

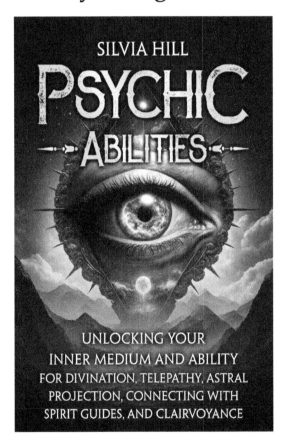

SILVIA HILL

PSYCHIC
ABILITIES

UNLOCKING YOUR
INNER MEDIUM AND ABILITY
FOR DIVINATION, TELEPATHY, ASTRAL
PROJECTION, CONNECTING WITH
SPIRIT GUIDES, AND CLAIRVOYANCE

Free Bonus from Silvia Hill available for limited time

Hi Spirituality Lovers!

My name is Silvia Hill, and first off, I want to THANK YOU for reading my book.

Now you have a chance to join my exclusive spirituality email list so you can get the ebooks below for free as well as the potential to get more spirituality ebooks for free! Simply click the link below to join.

P.S. Remember that it's 100% free to join the list.

~~$27~~ FREE BONUSES

- 9 Types of Spirit Guides and How to Connect to Them
- How to Develop Your Intuition: 7 Secrets for Psychic Development and Tarot Reading
- Tarot Reading Secrets for Love, Career, and General Messages

Access your free bonuses here
https://livetolearn.lpages.co/jewish-magic-paperback/

References

Ariel, D. S. (1977). The mystic quest: An introduction to Jewish mysticism. Jason Aronson, Incorporated.

Besserman, P. (2018). Kabbalah: The way of the Jewish mystic (Vol. 24). Shambhala Publications.

Blumenthal, D. R. (Ed.). (1978). Understanding Jewish mysticism: A source reader. KTAV Publishing House, Inc.

Elior, R. (2004). The Three Temples: On the Emergence of Jewish Mysticism. Liverpool University Press.

Frankiel, T., & Greenfeld, J. (1997). Minding the temple of the soul: Balancing body, mind, and spirit through traditional Jewish prayer, movement, and meditation. Jewish Lights Publishing.

Ginsburgh, R. Y. (1990). The Hebrew letters: Channels of creative consciousness (Vol. 1). GalEinai Publication Society.

Ginsburg, Y., Trugman, A. A., & Wisnefsky, M. Y. (1991). The Alef-Beit: Jewish Thought Revealed through the Hebrew Letters. Rowman & Littlefield.

Green, A. (2014). Keter: The Crown of God in Early Jewish Mysticism (Vol. 366). Princeton University Press.

Haralick, R. M. (1995). Inner Meaning of the Hebrew Letters. Jason Aronson, Incorporated.

Rowland, C., & Morray-Jones, C. R. (2009). The Mystery of God: Early Jewish Mysticism and the New Testament. Brill.

Schäfer, P. (2011). The origins of Jewish mysticism. Princeton University Press.

Schafer, P. (2012). Hidden and Manifest God, The: Some Major Themes in Early Jewish Mysticism. SUNY Press.

Scholem, G. (1967). Jewish mysticism. Merkabah Mysticism and Talmudic Tradition

Printed in Great Britain
by Amazon

40634167R00069